DON'T SCREW UP YOUR DIVORCE

How to be fully prepared and avoid costly mistakes

Sharing answers to your 8 biggest concerns

Chloe Oudiz

First edition
ISBN: 978-1-0683296-0-9

Enquiries: chloe@thedivorceandseparationcoach.com
Website: www.thedivorceandseparationcoach.com

Furthermore, the advice contained in this book is not intended to apply to couples with a history of domestic abuse. If your spouse has been violent, controlling or verbally abusive towards you, I urge you to speak to a specially trained professional who can focus first and foremost on ensuring your and your children's safety. Please visit my website for names of charities who can provide immediate help and support.

Cover images: Canva/Adobe Firefly
Published by CLMO Consulting Ltd

"If you only ever read only one book about divorce, make it this one." IAN LOVATT, FAMILY MEDIATOR

"Before you do anything, read this book! It will make all the difference to how you approach the process and the overall outcome for you and your family." ANNA SHARP, DIVORCE FINANCIAL ADVISER

"A must-read for anyone looking to avoid common mistakes and stay organised." AMBAR BHARWANI, FAMILY LAWYER

"An excellent, clear and concise, go-to guide for anyone contemplating the difficult journey of divorce." MELISSA LESSON, FAMILY LAWYER

"An invaluable step by step guide to a process many people find among the most daunting experiences of their life." PETER BURGESS, FAMILY LAWYER

"Clear, concise and incredibly empowering." PAULA CROWHURST, DIVORCE COACH

"Chloe guides her readers thoughtfully and compassionately through a version of separation in which cooperation, communication and ultimately, success, are all possible." ANNE HEATON-ARMSTRONG, PSYCHOTHERAPIST

"From myth-busting assumptions and perceptions to offering a more positive way through the process, it's like you're talking to a friend who has no agenda but yours." ANNIE RODGERS, CAREER COACH

Dedication

To my mother, who spent countless hours reading and advising me on this book. Thank you for always giving me your all.

To my father, for his steady and unconditional support.

To my friends, family and colleagues without whom this book would never have come to life.

Table of contents

"By failing to prepare, you are preparing to fail"

Benjamin Franklin

Introduction

Why didn't someone tell me all this before? Why didn't someone tell me how important it was to prepare for my divorce and help me avoid the many mistakes I made? Some of these mistakes are still costing me dearly today, ten years on. That is why I am writing this book. If I can help even one person avoid some of the biggest mistakes I and so many others have made, then I will have fulfilled my objective.

In this first book, I will focus on one of the most essential lessons I have learned: the importance of preparing sufficiently prior to initiating your divorce. I cannot overstate the value of taking your time before proceeding with this major decision. A reflection period will provide you with two invaluable commodities: the time to prepare emotionally for the journey ahead and life afterwards, and the time to gather information and develop a clear plan of action. Unfortunately, I did not take the time to do either of these. This played a large part in me subsequently training to become a Certified Divorce Coach®, and now writing this book.

Many of my clients enter my office having decided to leave their spouse, or they have just been told that their spouse is leaving them but have no idea of what to do next. There is a moment of feeling like a rabbit in the headlights, facing the enormity of the situation but unable to proceed because all options are equally scary. This is where taking the time to stop and think things through is essential. In these early stages, the work I do with my clients is not focused on negotiation strategies or co-parenting, which come later. It is specifically centred around the art of preparing efficiently and appropriately. So, if you are feeling like that rabbit in the headlights right now, I've got you!

The following pages have been written specifically to provide you with practical information that will help you prepare properly and enter the divorce process with your eyes wide open. I have structured this book around eight essential questions that most of us are concerned about when we are deciding how to proceed with the decision to divorce:

1. Are my fears and assumptions about divorce true?
2. How do I avoid starting a war?
3. What are my options for divorce?
4. How do I get organised?
5. Can I afford to divorce?
6. How do I tell my spouse and children?
7. How do I tell others?
8. What happens next?

By tackling each of these primordial concerns, this book will help you regain a sense of control over an overwhelming and frightening situation. This roadmap to preparing for divorce will not only avoid you making painful mistakes, it will also save you money on unnecessary legal fees and reduce the overall stress related to your family's breakup. Taking the time to prepare will provide the added benefit of allowing you to think through the implications of your decision, to ensure that you are fully aware of the road ahead and of your long-term objectives.

Before we dive into the topic at hand, I would like to take a minute to note from the very start of this book that I am in no way an advocate for divorce. Believing that a divorce coach promotes divorce is like saying a doctor promotes illness. Divorce is a reality in our society today, whether my services exist or not. My objective is to help people adopt a family-centric approach to divorce, so it moves away from being a traumatic and destructive life event towards becoming an act of self-love and an opportunity for a happier life. For some of my clients, divorce is not the answer. I strongly encourage all couples who are facing difficulties to give it their all, especially if they have children. But life is too short to stay in an unhappy marriage and when people truly believe they have reached the end of the road, the best solution for everyone is to part ways in the most dignified and least painful manner possible. This is what this book is intended to help you do.

My personal divorce journey

My divorce story is a tale of two radically different experiences across three different countries. It all started in a traditional way, with my ex-husband and I meeting at university in New York. Six years later, we were living in London. We got married and I quickly became pregnant with our first daughter. Nineteen months after that seismic change, I gave birth to our second daughter. As we settled into our new life as parents, our relationship grew increasingly strained, with both of us feeling more like roommates than partners. We were caught in a cycle of resentment, frustration, and unmet expectations. The decision to divorce wasn't easy — it was born out of exhaustion and the painful realisation that we were better off apart than together.

When we finally reached the conclusion that divorce was the best option, it was a bittersweet moment. There was no joy in it, but there was a sense of relief, as if we were finally releasing each other from a relationship that had become a source of constant stress. Our conversations were fraught with emotions—anger, sadness, guilt—but somehow, amid all the turmoil, we managed to keep things civil enough to move forward. It helped that we didn't have any property or significant assets to divide, and we both earned about the same amount of money, which simplified the financial aspect of the divorce. But even then, there were moments when our discussions nearly derailed, and it was hard to continue negotiating rather than bringing out the big guns.

Eventually, after many difficult conversations and a lot of compromise, we managed to reach an agreement. In a strained but co-operative effort, we spent a relatively small amount of money to finalise everything. Of course, this doesn't mean that the divorce wasn't psychologically taxing or that neither of us worried about ending up alone. The emotional unpacking of the end of a marriage usually takes time, and we were no exception. Nonetheless, we made the most out of an unpleasant situation. Both of us chose to stay in London post-divorce and my ex moved into a house down the street.

We each began the next chapter of our lives, but the transition took time for all of us to get used to. There were awkward encounters, tense exchanges, and moments when the wounds of our past felt too fresh to truly move on. Still, we managed to maintain a functional relationship, mostly for the sake of our children, but also because deep down, we both knew that holding on to bitterness would only make things harder for everyone involved.

Co-parenting after divorce is not an easy exercise, especially when it turns out you have such different parenting styles and values. Every decision felt like a negotiation and old frustrations re-emerged. There were days when I dreaded speaking to my ex because I knew it would stir up unpleasant feelings in me. Nonetheless, life went on and we started to find a new equilibrium. The children progressively settled into their new life and were happy to have easy access to both of us on a regular basis.

But then, life took an unexpected turn, leading to my second experience with divorce negotiations —one that was far more painful and complicated. After five years of relatively stable co-parenting, my ex-husband suddenly left England to live overseas. We were both long-time expats so there was always a possibility that one of us would move to another country. But I certainly never expected it to happen without us discussing and planning the consequences of the move, especially for our children. This unexpected turn of events created a new distance in our relationship, both physically and emotionally.

This time around, the situation was anything but straightforward. The lines of communication and trust, which had always been fragile, now completely broke down. We were thrust into a complex legal battle that felt never-ending. Jurisdictional issues added layers of challenges. I will spare you the technical details, but it is easy to understand how complicated the situation became and how fast legal fees accumulated across three different countries. The absurdity of the situation was that we didn't even need a court to step in, we simply needed to speak to each other to find a new arrangement that aligned with our new circumstances.

Indeed, what really made this second iteration of our divorce so painful was the total lack of co-operation and understanding between us. Poor advice from lawyers, friends and family led us to dig our heels in and to stop all direct communication. Nasty correspondence, compounded with emotionally damaging court hearings, further increased the divide between us. We were both consumed by our own anger and frustration, unable to see past our immediate disagreements. It felt like we were throwing money into a black hole, all because we couldn't bring ourselves to sit down and talk things through. However, the worst consequence of the legal quagmire was the damage done to our relationship as co-parents. Our collaboration, already fragile from years of strain, was now completely broken.

In the end, after months of exhausting negotiations, we finally reached an agreement on both the financial consequences of this change and the new child arrangements.

Alongside the many mistakes I made sits the overall regret of having handled this conflict so poorly. Thankfully, with all mistakes comes a number of learnings, which I am now sharing with you in this book. My two personal experiences with divorce taught me more about myself and my capacity for resilience than I ever could have imagined. The initial divorce, while difficult, showed me the importance of communication and compromise, even when it feels impossible. The second was a harsh reminder of how quickly things can fall apart when trust and co-operation are lost. Both experiences have left their mark on me, shaping who I am today and reminding me of the importance of fostering trust and communication, even when it feels like the hardest thing in the world.

Five years have come and gone since all this happened and it took me a large part of those years to let go of the resentment I felt towards my ex. We are now at a stage where we are able to behave in a civil manner when we need to collaborate on matters pertaining to the children, and that might just be all we need.

Becoming a Divorce coach

We all know the expression "when life gives you lemons, make lemonade!". This is precisely what I chose to do. Leveraging the wealth of knowledge I had acquired through my personal journey, and the invaluable experience of both amicable and litigated divorce, I began to help others going through their own separation. This all happened quite organically, with friends and colleagues approaching me about their marital problems. Because my children had been so young when my ex-husband and I split, I was often the only divorced person they knew. People around me came to me for advice, information or simply a shoulder to cry on. I listened, helped them shape their strategy and shared lessons from my own experience. As time went on, friends started putting me in contact with other people they knew who were struggling with their divorce. I became the divorce expert in my community and a go-to person for support.

At that time, I had been working for a large consulting firm for many years. I was a senior leader in the Global part of the organisation. I had extensive experience in change management and the psychology of change, both of which were immensely valuable skill sets when guiding people through divorce. But I was feeling more and more that the corporate world was no longer meant for me. I had lost all sense of purpose and felt increasingly burned out by the constant pressure and promotion cycles.

The decision to launch my coaching practice and make it a full-time activity was not an easy one to make. Although it was clear to me that

I was getting enormous fulfilment and satisfaction from helping others directly, I was also operating as a single mother with no financial safety net. I had to decide whether to follow my heart or my fears. In an exciting leap of faith, I decided to quit my corporate job and become a full-time divorce and separation coach. I chose to complete the CDC Certified Divorce Coach® programme to complement my previous education and experience so that I could provide my clients with the highest quality service possible. As a Conflict Management and Alternative Dispute Resolution expert, I support my clients through the incredibly challenging life transition that is divorce.

The vast majority of my clients come to see me at a stage when they have just decided to divorce but aren't too sure what to do next. My job is to help them set themselves up for success by negotiating their divorce settlement out of court. This allows them to divorce faster, with less conflict, and with reduced emotional and financial strain. It is an honour for me to be able to accompany my clients as their guide through the ups and downs of divorce, and to ensure their settlements provide them with security and appropriate outcomes.

Due to my own international background – I am a Franco-American living in London - and personal experience with divorce across multiple jurisdictions, I have naturally gravitated towards supporting expatriate families, of which there are many in a country as cosmopolitan as England. While I also work with many individuals who are divorcing in their home country, I provide an additional level of expertise to those who are living abroad.

Both expat and bi-national couples face a number of challenges that go beyond a traditional breakup. These include, among other things, questions about the possible relocation of one parent with or without the children, jurisdiction decisions, immigration implications, tax considerations and many other specificities that need to be considered as part of their divorce settlement. Additionally, they face an extremely stressful, life-changing experience without their family or usual support system nearby, while having to understand a foreign legal system in a language that is often not their native tongue. Many of my clients have followed their spouse abroad and deprioritised their career as a consequence. They are therefore particularly vulnerable with regards to financial stability and the lack of social safety nets.

In this context, having specialised professional support is essential to ensure qualified guidance through all the complexities and implications of ending an international marriage. I therefore connect my clients to an eclectic and multi-lingual network of specialised professionals around the world who have particular expertise in cross-border divorces: financial planners, lawyers, family mediators, psychotherapists, immigration lawyers and tax advisers, among others.

Alongside the more generic advice offered throughout this book, you will therefore notice that I highlight some specific information and guidance targeted at international families.

The purpose of this book

By guiding my clients through the preparatory phases of their divorce, I empower them to take control of events and to navigate their separation in the most efficient way possible. The time invested in this initial stage is not only worthwhile, it is essential. As you will see in this book, there are many steps that need to be taken prior to starting any part of the legal process. Because divorce is first and foremost a life experience, treating it as such will avoid the pitfall of turning it into a legal exercise.

When I speak of "preparation", I am including both logistical and emotional readiness. Because divorce is so overwhelming, many of my clients are tempted to hire a lawyer and delegate the process to them. In many ways, this is the most comfortable option: it avoids having to make any decisions yourself and it creates a buffer between you and your ex. A lawyer, however, is trained to handle the legal aspects of divorce, not to prepare and guide you through the personal dimensions of this life transition, no matter how empathetic they are. For better or worse, you are likely to have many other discussions with your ex even after the divorce is finalised, especially if you have children together. Hiding behind a lawyer is neither a sustainable solution nor an economically viable one.

Don't get me wrong, lawyers absolutely have a place in the divorce process. They are essential advisers with regards to the legal implications of the decisions you will be making. But in the same way you don't ask your surgeon to do the physiotherapy after an operation, you cannot expect your lawyer to provide support with regards to the non-legal aspects of your divorce if they are not trained to do so.

Coming back to the question I asked at the very start of this book, I aim to be the "someone" who told you about the importance of preparing for your divorce and helped you avoid costly mistakes. While there are unfortunately a multitude of miscalculations that can end up costing you dearly, there are three main actions you can choose to take to smooth your divorce journey:

- Take time to prepare.
- Enter the process with the right mindset and your eyes wide open.
- Surround yourself with the right people to ensure you are getting appropriate support.

I will cover these in more detail in the upcoming chapters.

Chapter 1: Are my fears and assumptions about divorce true?

In a nutshell

1. Divorce does not need to be a war where one person wins and the other loses.
2. Your ability to negotiate divorce settlements out of court will have a big impact on your overall experience and that of your children.
3. There is no such thing as emotional justice in divorce proceedings.

Like many themes that have been heavily addressed in movies, television and books, divorce is often misunderstood. This is in large part because the laws of divorce are constantly evolving and vary considerably from one country to the next. As attitudes and the stigma of divorce continue to evolve, so do laws and legal precedents. But myths and legends about divorce also continue to prevail due to the dramatic portrayal of divorce in the media. Movies such as *"Kramer vs Kramer"*, *"War of the Roses"* or *"Divorce Story"* consistently portray divorce as a war-like process where the parties' interests are inevitably opposed and chaos looms. In most cases, one of the two spouses is depicted as the only wrongdoer while the other is a victim. The image this gives of an experience nearly a third of British couples now face is not only misleading, it is dangerous. [1] In this section of the book, I would like to take a step back and correct some of the most common misconceptions about divorce.

This chapter could easily become its own book so, for the sake of conciseness, I will focus on the most common divorce myths I encounter:

1. Divorce always requires an expensive legal battle.
2. Getting a divorce is going to hurt my children.
3. Mothers always get custody of the children.
4. My spouse is going to take everything away from me.
5. A judge will see my side of the story and "punish" my spouse.

---

[1] According to the Office of National Statistics, the average overall divorce rate stands at 31.8%, considering all marriages from 1964 to 2019.

Myth: Divorce always requires an expensive legal battle

While divorces can indeed become costly, especially when disputes over finances or children arise, this is not an inevitable outcome. Although it is obviously not the case everywhere in the world, many Western countries have greatly simplified the divorce process in order to decongest the courts and make the transition simpler. In England & Wales for example, divorce is, at its core, a legal process that can be straightforward, particularly when both parties agree to the terms of the separation. The law allows individuals to handle the divorce themselves, without the need for a lawyer. This process, often referred to as a "DIY divorce", is not only possible but is also increasingly common, especially in cases where the divorce is uncontested.[2] In a similar spirit, French law offers couples an option to divorce without the intervention of a judge by simply asking a *notaire* to record the agreements their lawyers have documented, although each party is required to have their own lawyer.

---

[2] The information provided with regards to laws in various jurisdictions was correct at the time of writing this book. Beware as laws may have changed since. Always consult a lawyer to verify local laws and regulations.

"Divorce doesn't have to be a battle. It can just be the end of something, a sad but necessary thing. It doesn't have to be about blame, or fighting over everything; sometimes it's just about letting go, quietly."

"The Break" by Marian Keyes

The key to saving money and reducing conflict is to avoid litigation. The cost of hiring lawyers, expert witnesses and forensic accountants often stems from the spiral of conflict in which the spouses get caught up. As governments grow increasingly aware of the pitfalls of litigating family matters, many countries have been pushing for the use of Non-Court Dispute Resolution (NCDR) options such as family mediation, collaborative law or sharing a lawyer.[3] Similarly, divorce coaching is officially recognised in the United States by the American Bar Association as a form of Alternative Dispute Resolution and is encompassed in the April 2024 changes to the Financial Procedure Rules in England & Wales. As laws and judicial procedures evolve towards a less litigious approach to divorce, these forms of negotiation support are being increasingly encouraged by the courts. There are now, more than ever, a multitude of options available to divorcing couples who are struggling to reach an agreement but are trying to avoid going to court.

---

[3] See Chapter 3 for details on each of these options. Please note that not all NCDR options are available in all jurisdictions and that the agreements you reach may not be recognised as valid in every country.

As a result, more and more divorces are being resolved amicably, without lengthy, stressful and costly litigation. It is time for us to reframe the narrative around divorce to move away from the conflictual depiction we usually see. While divorce will never be a painless or conflict-free process, there are many shades of grey between staying married and going to war with your spouse.

DID YOU KNOW?

You can change your mind! In England & Wales, you can cancel divorce proceedings prior to the final order if both parties agree. You will have to write to the court and explain why you want to withdraw the petition. If the petition has been served on your spouse, you will need their consent or the court's permission to dismiss it. If you reconcile after the Conditional Order (formerly called Decree Nisi), you can ask the court to rescind the decree and dismiss the petition[4].

[4] As noted above, laws can change with the passing of time, so it is vital to consult a lawyer who is based in the jurisdiction involved.

Myth: Getting a divorce is going to hurt my children

I cannot tell you how often my clients share that their biggest fear is hurting their children by getting divorced. Children are, however, remarkably resilient and can adapt to change when they are provided with a stable and supportive environment. The notion that divorce automatically leads to long-term psychological harm in children is outdated and oversimplified. Research going back to the 1980s suggests that it is not the divorce itself, but the level of conflict and hostility between parents before, during, and after the separation that has the most significant impact on children's wellbeing.[5]

When parents engage in ongoing arguments, display bitterness, or speak negatively about one another in front of their children, tension and animosity become a daily reality for the child. This environment of conflict can cause anxiety, insecurity and emotional turmoil, leading to issues such as low self-esteem, behavioural problems, and difficulties in forming healthy relationships later in life. The child may feel torn between two parents, struggling with loyalty conflicts and the fear of losing the love of one or both parents.

---

[5] Surviving the Breakup: How Children and Parents Cope with Divorce. By Judith S. Wallerstein and Joan Berlin Kelly. New York: Basic Books, 1980.

In contrast, when parents manage their divorce amicably, prioritising their children's emotional needs and maintaining a co-operative relationship, the children are far less likely to experience severe emotional difficulties. Don't get me wrong, children are also deeply affected by divorce, as they often experience it as a form of loss. They, too, need support as they navigate their grief[6]. However, an atmosphere of respect and open communication can help children feel secure and loved, even as their family structure changes. When children see that their parents can still co-operate and co-parent effectively, they are more likely to adjust well and feel confident that they are not the cause of the separation.

USEFUL STATISTIC

According to a study by Custody X Change conducted in the US in September 2024, parents who get along post-divorce are 53% more likely to say their children have adjusted well.

---

[6] Working with a child psychologist can be invaluable in helping children process their feelings during this period.

Myth: Mothers always get to keep the children

The notion that the mother should be the children's primary care giver is becoming more and more obsolete. Over the past decade, there has been a marked shift towards more balanced parenting schedules, reflecting the growing awareness that children benefit most when both parents are actively involved in their lives.

In the past, mothers were more likely to be granted primary care of the children due to traditional gender roles and assumptions about the father's ability and inclination to spend significant time with his children. As society has evolved, so has the understanding that fathers play an equally crucial role in raising children. We are seeing this evolution reflected in the judicial system, with family courts becoming more inclined to favour shared parenting arrangements where both parents have significant time with their children.

In England & Wales, as in many other countries, the guiding principle for judges issuing child arrangement orders is to prioritise the best interests of the children. This means that decisions are based not on outdated stereotypes, but on what will best support the child's physical, emotional, and psychological needs. When making decisions about child arrangements, judges consider several factors. These include the child's age, their relationship with each parent, the parents' ability to co-operate, and the child's wishes, depending on their age and maturity. The parent's gender is not a recognised factor in deciding on child arrangements.

What the court will do, however, is assess the stability and suitability of each parent's home environment, as well as any history of abuse or neglect. The focus is on ensuring that the child has a safe, stable, and loving environment, regardless of which parent provides it. The fear that many parents have during divorce - that they are going to "lose their children"- is absolutely unfounded unless there is a serious reason why the children are not safe in their care. Even in those cases, the courts usually do their best to maintain some form of contact with both parents, through supervised visitation or virtual calls. One of my clients recently called me in a panic because her husband had threatened to "take the children away from her" if she did not agree to the financial settlement he was proposing. Her lack of information on the subject (and his as well, probably) made her particularly vulnerable to these types of threats. It is, in fact, very rare for courts to find that it is against the children's interests to have both parents in their lives. Being aware of this fact is, therefore, a hugely powerful tool in this context.

Myth: My spouse is going to take everything from me

The notion that one spouse can take everything away from the other during a divorce is a common myth, often fuelled by sensationalised media portrayals and anecdotal horror stories. However, in many countries, this perception does not align with the reality of divorce proceedings.

Divorce law in Australia, as an example, is grounded in principles of a "just and equitable" division of assets upon divorce based on the Family Law Act 1975. The court's primary objective is to ensure a fair distribution of assets that takes into account the needs and contributions of both parties. It will consider factors such as the length of the marriage, the age and health of the spouses, and their respective financial resources. Just like in England & Wales, the law does not favour one party over the other but instead seeks to ensure that both spouses emerge from the divorce with an equitable share of the marital assets.

This myth is further debunked by the fact that prenuptial agreements, while not legally binding in every jurisdiction, are often influential in determining the division of assets. These agreements provide a measure of protection for both parties, making it less likely that one spouse could unilaterally claim all the assets. On the flip side, a prenuptial agreement that has been signed under pressure or that is grossly inequitable will often be rejected by the court, making it impossible for one spouse to "plan" to dispossess the other if they were to divorce.

The courts also consider the welfare of the children involved, prioritising their needs when dividing assets. This often results in arrangements that ensure both parents can adequately provide for their children post-divorce, rather than one spouse being left destitute.

Myth: A judge will see my side of the story and "punish" my spouse

This is a theme I already touched on when we discussed some of the main mindset shifts that need to occur before beginning the divorce process. I insist on this point because of the frequency with which I hear people voice this misconception. I cannot count the times when a client has expressed an interest in taking their divorce to court as in search of emotional justice. I fully relate to their need to be vindicated and to see the family court judge empathise with their plight, punishing the spouse for their poor behaviour during the marriage. This belief often stems from the emotional turmoil surrounding divorce, where one partner may feel wronged or believe that the other deserves retribution. However, the role of the family court is not to pass moral judgement or to punish spouses but instead to ensure that legal matters are resolved fairly and equitably. For the spouse who feels like they have been wronged, this can often be a very disappointing reality. Unfortunately for them, no matter how badly their spouse may have behaved, it is a fallacy to expect to receive emotional justice by going to court. As my own therapist once told me, "This is probably why so many religions believe in some version of karma".

Judges understand that relationships are complex and that assigning blame in the breakdown of a marriage is rarely straightforward. They do not base their decisions on who was a "good" or "bad" spouse. Instead, they focus on what is necessary to achieve a fair outcome. The concept of "fault" has even been largely removed from the divorce process with the introduction of "no-fault" divorces in many countries around the world. As an example, Germany passed a law allowing no-fault divorce in 1977. California became the first state to allow no-fault divorce in 1969 but has since been followed by all other US states. More recently, England & Wales removed all the behavioural facts that had been used to establish divorce in 2022, further emphasising that the court's role is not to assign blame.

This myth may persist because of the emotional weight that accompanies divorce, but it is important to recognise that family courts are institutions of law. The scenario where one party finally gets "their day in court" and sees the judge take their side to reprimand their spouse only exists in movies.

EXPERT TIP

One strategy which I have found very useful over the years, for myself and my clients, is to write a letter to a fictional jury. In this letter, you can share an uncensored version of what happened to you, including all the feelings you are grappling with. Imagine that you are in a court of law, and you are asked to state your case about why you feel you have been wronged. This letter, as you can expect, will not be sent to anyone, it will serve as an outlet for all the frustrations you haven't been able to express during a divorce process that does not account for emotional loss. It is quite remarkable how helpful it can be to get your thoughts out of your head and onto paper, to finally express them freely without fear of consequences.

The multitude of obsolete or erroneous ideas people still have about divorce is one of the main reasons why divorces can go wrong. When an individual is making decisions relating to their divorce based on wrong expectations, they are bound for disappointment and ill-advised decisions. This is why surrounding yourself with qualified and carefully selected professionals is essential. In the various dimensions of preparation for divorce outlined in this book, information gathering is the first and sometimes most significant step. Let's begin by exploring the details of what you need to know before initiating your divorce.

Chapter 2: How do I avoid starting a war?

In a nutshell

1. A negotiated out-of-court resolution will save you money, time and stress.
2. Take the time you need to process your feelings before kicking off the divorce.
3. Prepare yourself for your spouse's reaction by defining their go-to conflict style.

Ninety percent of couples begin their divorce process with the intention of keeping it amicable.[7] That is often because they want to avoid the conflict, cost and time it takes to divorce in court. Starting off with the right intentions is definitely a great place to begin, but divorce is a lot more like a marathon than a sprint. It is effectively a business negotiation similar to a corporate divestiture but with very high personal stakes. So how do you make sure you stay the course? You do so by ensuring that you are approaching the situation with the right expectations and in control of your emotions. Let's delve into what that involves, in practice.

Starting your divorce in the right state of mind

Going back to my analogy of divorce being like a marathon, you are defining what the finish line looks like from the start rather than running aimlessly towards an unknown goal. The role of a Certified Divorce Coach® is specifically to help you design that finish line and help you reach it. In order to do so, you need to be clear about what an achievable objective looks like for you. Is your objective to break a world record or

[7] A survey conducted by the U.K. family law service Amicable in 2021 revealed that 90% of respondents initially intended to divorce amicably, wishing to avoid conflict and court battles.

simply to finish? The answer will vary greatly from one person to the next and remains a deeply personal decision.

When it comes to preparing to take the first steps towards divorce, one of the most crucial things is to ensure you adopt the right mindset. In that regard, I strongly encourage my clients to make five major changes in their attitudes towards divorce. They must recognise that:

1. Out-of-court resolution leads to better outcomes.
2. Divorce is a forward-looking exercise.
3. Moral and emotional justice are not part of the process.
4. There is no such thing as entitlement.
5. Divorce isn't about their ex, it is about them.

(1) OUT-OF-COURT RESOLUTION LEADS TO BETTER OUTCOMES

In my first chapter, when we discussed misconceptions about divorce, I explained that it is wrong to believe that divorce necessarily entails a long and costly legal battle. I would like to correct here another related misconception: that amicable divorce is only an option when the spouses agree on everything. That is not the case, nor is it realistic to expect a couple to agree on absolutely everything. Every divorce involves conflict. By definition, assets and time with children are being split up, meaning both parties will feel a sense of loss. Very few couples manage to maintain a friendly relationship in this context. But getting along is absolutely not a pre-requisite to divorcing out of court. Spouses don't need to be best friends, they don't even need to like each other. Even more surprising, they don't even need to speak to each other directly! What allows people to negotiate an agreement without litigation is a commitment to maintaining control of the conversation rather than asking a judge to make the decision for them. This commitment requires resilience and an ability to think creatively when negotiations come to a standstill.

MISTAKE #1: DELEGATING THE DECISION TO A JUDGE WITHOUT ATTEMPTING TO NEGOTIATE FIRST

There is no denying that negotiating the terms of your future life at the same time as you are facing some of the most stressful transitions you have ever experienced is a challenge. While asking a third party such as a judge to make these decisions for you can be incredibly tempting, achieving a resolution out of court brings undeniable advantages. By divorcing amicably, you will be preserving your own and your children's wellbeing by limiting stress, conflict and uncertainty. If you are co-parenting, this means you will ultimately find it easier to work together as a team to raise your children going forward and have a much better post-divorce relationship.

A low-conflict divorce will also likely help you achieve a better outcome because it will be one that you agreed to willingly, after careful consideration, not one that was dictated by a third party who doesn't know you.

Unfortunately, the idea that divorce is a war where someone loses and someone wins still dominates mindsets. The reality is that everyone will lose a little and win a little. But when you go to court and turn the process into an open conflict, everybody loses, including your children and your bank account.

"In divorce, there is no winning... only degrees of losing."

Danny De Vito, The War of the Roses

② DIVORCE IS A FORWARD-LOOKING EXERCISE

Divorce is fundamentally a forward-looking exercise, a process focused on closing one chapter and laying the groundwork for a new one. The process of divorce, when approached constructively, is less about dwelling on the past and more about shaping the path ahead.

At its core, divorce is a family restructuring that necessitates clarity and foresight. While it is natural for emotions tied to the experiences of the marriage to arise, the divorce process is primarily focused on what comes next. The decisions you will be making —whether related to finances, children, or personal wellbeing— are fundamentally about ensuring that your post-divorce future is stable, secure and conducive to personal growth.

Don't get me wrong, processing emotions from the marriage is important, but it is a separate, independent journey. The healing and reflection needed to move past the emotional repercussions of the relationship are essential. As is the need to grieve the relationship you once had and the joint future you had envisioned. I have seen many clients unable to effectively begin divorce negotiations because they hadn't taken the time to heal from the grief, hurt or guilt associated with it. Despite the importance of emotional processing, one must understand that the legal process of divorce is not the arena for this. Instead, the legal procedure was developed as a mechanism for creating new boundaries, responsibilities and opportunities. It involves making decisions that will define the next chapter, from financial arrangements to living situations, all of which will play a crucial role in the rebuilding process.

To keep this forward momentum in play, it is crucial to stay away from blaming and revisiting past behaviours in conversations with your soon-to-be-ex. Reliving past conflicts can significantly hinder your healing, drawing energy away from the essential task of building a stable and positive future.

When blame enters the dialogue, it often escalates tensions and reopens wounds, making it difficult to reach agreements amicably. Instead of fostering co-operation, it creates an adversarial environment that can prolong the divorce, increase emotional distress, and lead to more contentious legal battles. This, in turn, diverts attention from the constructive aspects of divorce, such as negotiating fair settlements, ensuring the wellbeing of children, and planning for independent futures.

"When emotions run high,
intelligence runs low."

Douglas Horton[8]

Focusing on the past can also cloud judgement, making it harder to see the bigger picture and to make decisions that serve long-term interests. The energy spent on rehashing old arguments could be better invested

[8] Douglas Horton (1891–1968) was an influential American Congregationalist clergyman, theologian, and religious leader.

in constructive discussions about practical matters—finances, child arrangements, and personal growth. By keeping conversations future-oriented and solution-focused, both parties can work towards outcomes that are beneficial for everyone involved, especially if children are part of the equation.

The emphasis should remain on what you need to move forward and rebuild your life, unencumbered by the weight of past grievances.

3 MORAL AND EMOTIONAL JUSTICE ARE NOT PART OF THE PROCESS

As we discussed in Chapter 1 regarding myths, the process has little to do with moral fairness. Many people see divorce through the lens of emotional justice, where one might expect a sense of moral victory or retribution for improper behaviour exhibited by their spouse during the marriage. This is why advice from friends and family can be unhelpful if it is focusing on what is morally right. Unfortunately for those who feel wronged, the legal process of divorce is primarily concerned with the formal dissolution of the marital contract. The legal system is not designed to address the emotional wounds inflicted during a marriage. Courts focus on facts, legal rights, and responsibilities rather than the subjective feelings of the parties. A typical example is when one spouse feels like the other should not be given as much access to the children because they cheated. In their mind and heart, it feels like the person "responsible" for the end of the marriage should come out with worse outcomes than the "victim".

THE LEGAL IMPLICATIONS OF INFIDELITY

"When someone believes their marriage has ended as a result of infidelity, they may feel that, as the injured party, they should receive a more generous financial settlement. Traditionally people believe that the unfaithful party will be treated more harshly in court. However, this is no longer true in England & Wales. In nearly all cases, the judge will not try to blame or penalise either party, except in very rare circumstances. For example, if one party's infidelity has financial implications, such as the dissipation of assets to fund extramarital affairs, then the court may take this into account when determining a fair financial settlement."

Ambar Bharwani, Solicitor at Expatriate Law

Watch the full podcast on how new romantic relationships impact divorced families on my You Tube channel:

(4) THERE IS NO SUCH THING AS ENTITLEMENT

Have you ever heard of the "divorce swear words"? I'm pretty sure they are not the ones you expect! These three words are: right, deserve, and entitled. I always encourage my clients to refrain from using these words, as they are truly counter-productive in the context of a divorce. As I have already explained, entering a successful negotiation requires a shift in mindset. Right and wrong have no place in a divorce because they are very relative concepts. What seems right to one person will not seem so to another.

The words "deserve" and "entitled" are also to be avoided. Many people believe the law dictates the terms of their divorce. Unfortunately, the reality is that every case is different, in particular in Common Law countries such as the UK and the US. Often, each party firmly believes that they have specific rights to certain things, whether it is to have the children most of the time because they are still young, or to receive half of their spouse's pension. Thinking in this manner sets unrealistic expectations and makes negotiations very difficult because everyone tends to dig their heels in based on what they think they deserve or are entitled to. If both parties have very firm expectations of what they should obtain, there is a strong chance there will not be any overlap between their two positions.

If the words "right, "deserve" and "entitled" are swear words in divorce, then what are the right words to use? In reality, divorce is about reaching an agreement that is both "reasonable" and "liveable" for both parties, and mutually satisfactory. It really isn't about what each person might get if they went to court, which is often hard to predict anyway. It is about what feels acceptable to them because it meets their top priorities and allows them to move on.

5 DIVORCE ISN'T ABOUT YOUR SOON-TO-BE-EX, IT IS ABOUT YOU

One of the transitions I see my clients struggle with most is the evolution from thinking as a couple to thinking as an individual. For years, perhaps decades, couples learn to make decisions that accommodate each other's needs and consider the implications of all their decisions on each other, and rightly so. During divorce, a monumental change needs to occur in each individual's psyche: the decisions they are making are no longer about their spouse, they are about themselves and their children. Because their lives will ultimately get untangled, both spouses need to start planning their own life at this stage, independently from the other. The decisions they make during the divorce will have long term implications which will be relevant to them and them only.

"Relationships, no matter how good, are inevitably a series of compromises. But how much of ourselves should we be willing to sacrifice for the other person before we stop being ourselves?"

Sarah-Jessica Parker in Sex and the City

The importance of developing personal goals should once again be highlighted here. The decisions that you make should be considered in relation to these goals. This means that no decisions will be made with the purpose of spiting your ex-spouse or seeking revenge. Nor will decisions be made based on what might annoy them most or on tit for tat. They will solely be evaluated with regards to whether they align with your values and your personal life objectives.

Here is a situation I encountered with a client recently:

A man contacted me for advice because his wife had left him. They had already begun the divorce process and were talking about dividing assets. He knew that what she cared about most was keeping the country house in which they vacationed each year. In negotiating the divorce settlement, he had chosen to deny her proposals to keep the house. He felt that she did not deserve to "win" this dispute because she was the one who had ended the marriage. I tried to help him look at the proposal she was making based on how it aligned with his own goals. His long-term objective was to retire at 65 and have a comfortable pension based on the contributions he had made throughout his career. Eventually he understood that it really didn't matter if his wife got her way and kept the country house, as long as he got what he wanted most, ie his pension. This doesn't mean that money is more important that emotions. It means that you shouldn't let emotions cloud the right decision for you: my client's main priority was to retire at 65 at the latest. He decided that his interest in "winning" ultimately meant less to him than this personal objective.

I am not suggesting here that divorce is a selfish process. Your children should always be the first priority in all the decisions you make. Your ex's wellbeing also matters, firstly because they are your children's other parent but also simply because they are a human being. But your interests must sit firmly ahead of your ex's at this stage. Your lives will slowly become less and less connected, and you will soon learn to live your life as solely yours. This process begins on the day you inform your spouse of your decision to split up and will progressively continue until you both move on from your marriage fully. This is one of the transitions that many of my clients find most difficult. I cannot tell you how many people have told me that they could not think of a life after marriage because they don't remember what matters to them. Their decision-making is so intertwined with considerations about the impact it will have on their spouse that they have forgotten how to make decisions for themselves. As an example, one of my clients told me that her life objective was to live as far away from her ex-husband as possible. While I can completely relate to the need to put some physical distance between yourself and someone who has hurt you, this is no longer the time to let your life be dictated by what the other is doing. She should be deciding where to settle based on her own ambitions, not to escape her husband. Keep in mind that over time, your divorce will feel less and less painful and that you do not want to be making long-term decisions based on short-term emotions.

I am fully aware that this is far easier said than done. We live in a society where we are constantly comparing ourselves to others, to the lives they display on social media, the size of their house or their professional successes. Defining your own standards of what constitutes happiness, independently of other people, is truly the key to personal satisfaction. In the context of divorce, this means letting go of your connection to your spouse and accepting that your lives are now separate. This is by far one of the hardest and longest transitions I see my clients work through and I remember struggling with this new framing as well.

EXPERT TIP

Here is an exercise that I have found particularly useful for my clients who are struggling to divorce emotionally from their soon-to-be-ex. If you find that you are still making decisions based on what your spouse liked, thought or said, it might be useful to take a formal step to say goodbye and move on. This can take the shape of an unsent letter or a conversation with yourself in the mirror. You could even do it with a friend who will play the role of your soon-to-be-ex in this scenario. Whatever form it takes, the idea is to say a formal goodbye. You are going to use this occasion to part ways emotionally with your spouse and give yourself permission to become independent from them. It is also important to take a moment to acknowledge some happy memories of the time you spent together. I encourage you to use your own words, but the essence of what you will be saying is: "We had some happy years and I hold many wonderful memories of our life together. The time has come for us to go our separate ways and today, I am saying goodbye to you. From this point forward you will no longer be a factor in my life decisions, and I will be moving forward based solely on what I feel is best for me. I wish you all the best in your own journey ahead". Once you have done that, try to start applying this new-found autonomy and making small day-to-day decisions based on your preferences only: choose an outfit that makes you happy no matter what your soon-to-be-ex would have thought of it, or go to a restaurant that you've always wanted to try even if your ex would have hated it. Little by little, you will see that this new way of thinking will become more comfortable, and you will be able to apply it to bigger decisions over time.

Emotional preparation

(1) YOUR OWN EMOTIONS

Emotional preparation involves becoming aware of one's feelings, managing stress, and developing a mindset conducive to constructive dialogue. This is essential before kicking off your divorce due to often deep-seated emotions and the complexity of past grievances and interactions. Entering the separation process without addressing these emotional components can hinder communication, exacerbate conflicts, and impede the negotiation process. This means that you should give yourself the time to grieve and heal prior to initiating the divorce as you will not be able to conduct level-headed conversations if emotions are too raw. Even if you are not the one who initiated the divorce, asking your spouse to slow things down so you have time to prepare for the road ahead is a reasonable request. It is also one that benefits them as well, as you will be a much more productive counterpart in the negotiations if you have had time to come to terms with your situation.

Similarly, taking time to reconnect with your true self and establish what you want to stand for is going to be hugely beneficial. In the midst of strong negative emotions, it isn't uncommon for people to lose track of their personal values. Anger, grief, jealousy and resentment are among the many feelings that cloud our judgement and lead us to behave in ways that we would usually feel embarrassed about. Friends and family, hoping to provide you with support, might even encourage these behaviours. Defining early on how you want to show up during the divorce negotiations, but also afterwards, will serve as a compass throughout the decision-making process. The question to ask yourself is: "If what I say or do was being filmed, would I be embarrassed?", or "How would I feel if my children saw a recording of how I have been behaving?".

Recently, one of my clients was advised by her lawyer to file for divorce in her home country in order to pre-empt her husband filing in England first. From a legal standpoint, she had more to win in getting divorced in France than she did in England and the advice made sense. However, she felt uncomfortable with this decision. When I asked her how this aligned with her values, she said she would feel like a total b***h if she were to do that without even telling her husband of 15 years that she wanted a divorce first. When asked about how she would feel if her children were to find out that she had initiated the divorce in this way, she said she would feel ashamed that she had treated their father this way. Together, we brainstormed a different approach: one that allowed her to show her husband the respect he deserved by informing him in person of her decision to divorce while securing the jurisdiction she favoured at the same time. This is a typical example of how your values can help you avoid mistakes and ensure you have no regrets later on. Incidentally, I had previously had a client who had been given the same advice but who had decided to do as she was being instructed. She ended up bitterly regretting her decision as her husband then refused to speak to her other than through lawyers and any chance of peaceful negotiations was lost.

It might seem like an unnecessary delay to begin by investing the time required to process emotions, but it almost certainly will end up saving you time and aggravation in the end. Most importantly, addressing divorce negotiations with a business-like mindset will make the entire process less painful and help you reach informed decisions that align to your future plans.

MISTAKE #2: JUMPING INTO NEGOTIATIONS BEFORE PROCESSING YOUR FEELINGS

I have helped many of my clients avoid committing this mistake. I remember vividly working with a man whose wife was determined to keep a small armchair they had bought during their honeymoon. While the armchair had some emotional value, it was probably worth £100 and was by no means irreplaceable. Before coming to see me, my client had been resisting his soon-to-be-ex's request for several weeks, making this one of the breaking points of the negotiations. Upon exploring the matter further, I realised that he personally had no specific attachment to the armchair, he felt it was a matter of principle: he didn't want his wife to feel like she had "won". Eventually, he realised that he was being driven by resentment and ego rather than rational thinking and that the cost of haggling over this armchair would ultimately be much greater than just letting his wife have it. Furthermore, if he had let her have it from the start, he might have built up a bit of goodwill on her part to get her to agree to one of his own requests. This is a typical example of how emotions can get in the way of a rational negotiation. Over the years, I have seen people go to war over such things as a tea set, a Lego collection or an additional hour of parenting time. These conversations, of course, have very little to do with the asset in dispute. They are due to the lack of emotional management that leads people to want to feel like they have come out on top. In some cases, it is also a way of not letting go of the relationship. No matter how toxic it may have become, giving in to that final request symbolises the final nail in the coffin of your marriage, and that can be a very frightening step to take.

(2) UNDERSTANDING YOUR SPOUSE'S CONFLICT STYLE

You may have heard about individual conflict styles[9] in the past. There are five major approaches to conflict. Take time early on to analyse your spouse's conflict style and gain awareness of your own. This will help you be more conscious of how they are likely to react and will allow you to work with your divorce coach to prepare your response to this reaction. There are many ways in which you can build an effective skillset to address

[9] Adapted from: Conflict Management Styles Descriptions. Docstoc, http://img.docstoccdn.com/thumb/orig/47081621.png

your spouse's conflict style in the most constructive way possible, while keeping the negotiations on track.

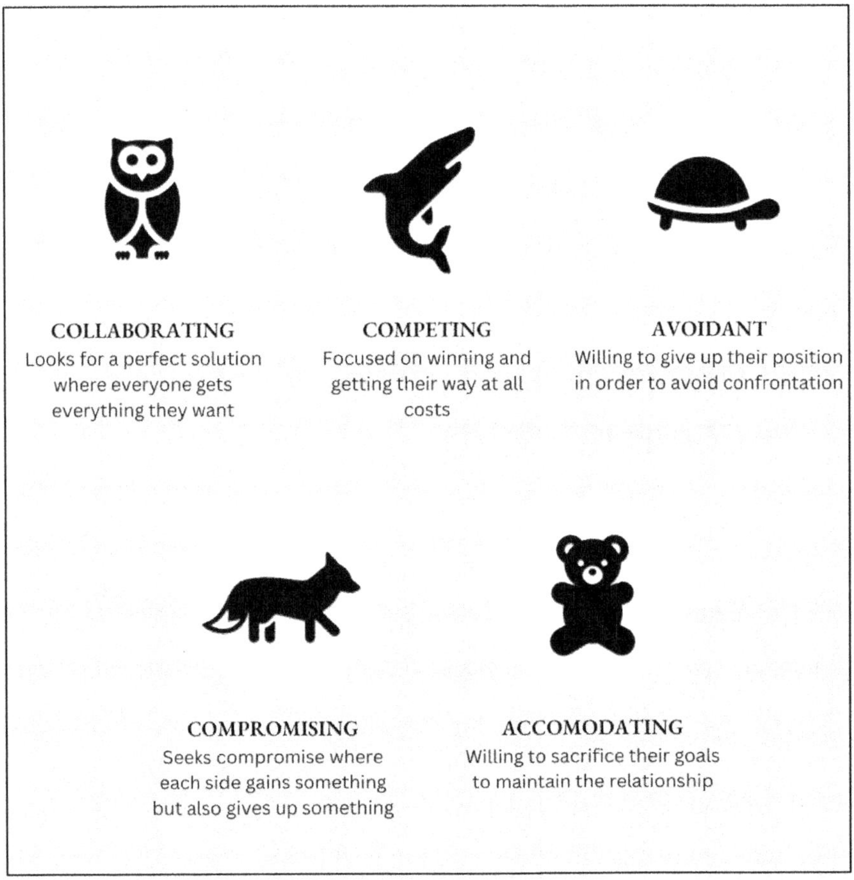

It should be pointed out from the start that every conflict style has its pros and cons. None of these are intrinsically the right or the wrong approach. For example, someone who tends to be accommodating might be very well liked by their friends, family and colleagues as they strive to make others happy and don't cause conflict. However, there is a strong chance they will eventually grow resentful from always being the one accommodating everyone else's needs.

With regards to divorce, collaborating and compromising tend to be the most helpful styles for resolving conflict as they are focused on seeking a joint solution. But your spouse's conflict style does not pre-determine how the divorce will unfold. Whatever your spouse's usual behaviour is during disagreements, you can prepare accordingly to help them join you at the negotiations table. Let's look at an example. Jane hates conflict and always leaves the room when she and her husband Hugh have an argument. Hugh correctly identifies that his wife has an avoidant conflict style but doesn't know what to do to bridge the gap in communication when she withdraws. Knowing how Jane operates, Hugh will need to tread carefully when discussing challenging topics and give Jane the space to express her views without fear of conflict breaking out. Using a calm tone of voice and reassuring her that the conversation will remain peaceful will be essential to ensure Jane opens up and communicates again. The context, timing and approach Hugh chooses to table difficult conversations will also need to be carefully thought through in order to keep the conflict level low and avoid Jane pulling away from the negotiations.

Alongside understanding your spouse's approach to conflict, being attentive to your own style will allow you to avoid escalation during disagreements. By being self-aware and recognising your own knee-jerk reactions to conflict, you can begin to adapt your communication approach to keep conversations productive. As an example, I know that I tend to be competing when something really matters to me. I like to feel that I am right. Being aware of this does not make me a different person – I will likely always be competing - but it helps me to control this tendency when it really matters. In my case, this means working hard to listen more to the other person's perspective, and acknowledging when they make a good point, even if I feel uncomfortable doing so. By doing this, I am more likely to find common ground with the other person and to find a mutually acceptable solution.

My clients often express interest in understanding both their own and their spouse's conflict styles, and they gain tremendous insights into the nature of their disagreements by doing so. These personality profiles are moulded over time, through nature itself and the personality we were born with, but also through nurture: our social class, gender, ethnicity, cultural influences, family history, past experiences and education, among other factors. The importance of what is at stake also greatly influences our individual conflict styles. With divorce being a threat to some of the things we hold dearest, it is not surprising that conflict styles often get exacerbated during this period.

In conclusion, before initiating a divorce, it is essential to arm yourself with both emotional and practical knowledge. Understand that divorce is not just an administrative formality but a profound emotional journey that will affect various aspects of your life. Being clear about your preferred approach to divorce, considering its potential impact on your children, finances and wellbeing, and having a support system in place are crucial first steps. Seeking advice from qualified professionals early on can help you make informed decisions, minimise conflict, and better navigate the challenges ahead.

Chapter 3: What are my options for divorce?

In a nutshell

1. There are many Non-Court Dispute Resolution options for you to choose from based on your situation, budget and priorities.
2. Where you get divorced can make a major difference, so do your research first.
3. Speak to several relevant professionals before deciding on the best route for your divorce.

One notable fact that many of my clients often don't realise is that divorce has many components. In most countries, divorce proceedings focus on three main elements:

- the legal recognition of the end of the marriage
- the division of matrimonial assets
- an agreement on child arrangements (when relevant).

This means that getting divorced isn't just about getting the end of the marriage officially documented, it is also about defining the terms of the divorce. In some jurisdictions, such as Switzerland, Italy or Japan, the financial and child arrangements are integrated into the legal process of getting a divorce by mutual consent: to get a divorce, you must also reach agreements on its consequences. In other countries, including most of the English-speaking world[10], couples can get legally divorced without having formal agreements with regards to their finances or children.

In this book, I refer to divorce in its broadest sense, that is to say, including both the legal recognition of the end of the marriage and the consequences of this with regards to finances and children. It is often these last two points that lead to the most conflict and end up creating some of the legal quagmires we see in the media.

---

[10] England & Wales, the United States, Australia and Canada among others

Understanding the different Non-Court Dispute Resolution pathways

As mentioned earlier, most countries are now trying to encourage out-of-court resolution of family conflicts. This is in large part because the courts are saturated, but also because judges have an understandable reluctance to make decisions that apply to the private realm of family life. Independently from these motivations, there are undeniable advantages to both the divorcing couple and their children in conducting negotiations with as little conflict as possible. One of the key learnings for me from the second iteration of my divorce was precisely that. While I fully expected that the litigated approach we opted for was going to lead to higher legal expenses, I grossly underestimated the psychological impact and stress of legal proceedings. My sleep was affected, as was my eating, and inevitably my moods. Even without the further costs involved and the negative impact it had on our co-parenting relationship, the stress alone scarred me to a point where I would never again engage in litigation, be it for professional or personal reasons. Today I would choose to leverage one of the many options for out-of-court dispute resolution and endeavour to find an agreement without the chaos of legal proceedings.

As many countries move in the direction of encouraging negotiated agreements out of court, the importance of Non-Court Dispute Resolution solutions is consistently rising. Before taking any concrete steps towards your divorce, I strongly recommend taking some time to understand the various options outlined below and assess their pros and cons. Getting early clarity on which method – or methods - might be most suited to your situation will allow you to approach your spouse with a concrete suggestion with regards to how the divorce process could unfold. But keep in mind that you can try different solutions if your initial idea doesn't work out. I have listed below some of the most common options that can be explored to reduce the costs and destruction of a litigated divorce. I have started with those that are likely to be the cheapest, ending with the usually most expensive. But keep in mind that all of these options are very likely to be cheaper than litigation. It is important to note that many jurisdictions are moving towards requiring or at least strongly encouraging some attempt at reaching agreements amicably before any type of court action can be initiated. However, not all the options listed below are available in all countries, so make sure you understand the specific NCDR options in your divorce jurisdiction. You should also consult a lawyer to confirm that both the divorce itself and your agreements will be recognised in other countries relevant to you. If you are still deciding which jurisdiction to file in, this will certainly be a factor to consider in your evaluation.

(1) DO-IT-YOURSELF DIVORCE

This requires sitting down with your spouse and ironing out the details of your separation between yourselves. This is definitely the cheapest way to proceed (as low as £640 vs the average £14,000 cost of divorce in the UK)[11] but it is not always the easiest. Both parties must be fully committed to finding solutions and willing to compromise. This is an ideal solution when the divorce is relatively "simple", ie there are limited assets and no children involved, though I have seen it done in more complicated situations as well. This approach means you must gather the right information on your own, document the arrangements yourselves and submit them to the court online. There are many low-cost services out there that can help you ensure everything is in order before submission, and some even handle the submission itself.

Speaking to a Certified Divorce Coach® can help you avoid some of the common mistakes and omissions, as well as get "unstuck" when there is a disagreement.

(2) FAMILY MEDIATION

I am a big fan of mediation, in large part because it is extremely flexible in its format, but also because it allows the couple to ask for external help while still remaining in control of their agreements, instead of delegating the decision to a third party.

---

[11] Aviva report on Family Finances Report: The hidden cost of divorce and separation, January 2018

A mediator is an independent, trained professional who works for the couple and helps them negotiate agreements for children or finances, though they cannot provide legal advice in the process. A mediator provides a neutral source of support in reaching viable agreements. These agreements are not legally binding, though, until they are turned into orders by a court of law. Mediators are usually less expensive than lawyers. The fact that he or she works for the couple rather than just one party helps keep costs under control and avoids the traditional "you vs me" approach. It is also a much faster process than taking your case to court: approximately six months on average vs 13 months for litigation.[12]

The beauty of family mediation is that it is incredibly flexible. It can take place online or in person, with both spouses in the same room or in separate rooms (this is called shuttle mediation, the mediator effectively goes back and forth between both parties), with or without lawyers/divorce coaches/therapists present. Mediation can also involve a session or two between the mediator and your children if they are old enough to share their opinion on the child arrangements. This is referred to as child-inclusive mediation. It helps give the children a voice in the decisions that impact them directly and provides them with a confidential forum to share their own preferences, without fear of upsetting their parents. It does require, however, both parents to agree to the children being heard.

---

12 New mediation laws to help separating couples, press release from the UK Ministry of Justice and The Rt Hon Lord McNally, published 5 June 2013

PODCAST ON FAMILY MEDIATION

In this episode, I was joined by Katy Harris, a qualified Family Law and Civil Mediator. Katy is the owner of Mediation Matters Midlands. As a trained and experienced family mediator, Katy talks us through the mediation process as well as the associated timelines and costs.

This podcast offers a window into the world of family mediation and how it works in practice. Scan the QR code to watch the video on You Tube:

Katy's three tips for successful mediation:

1- Come in with the right mindset, willing to negotiate and be creative.

2- Seek the right professional support during this negotiation.

3- Keep the wellbeing of your children at the centre of your considerations, no matter what your feelings towards your ex.

It is important to underline that mediation requires both parties to agree to it in order to proceed. If it fails, you will be left with the alternative of working with a different mediator or seeking a new approach to resolve your conflicts. Be aware that in some jurisdictions, such as Australia, mediation is a mandatory step before going to court on certain aspects of the divorce. Other countries, such as England, might not mandate attending mediation but will require an explanation as to why it hasn't been attempted.

Working with a Certified Divorce Coach® can prove particularly beneficial during mediation as they will help you prepare for meetings and define your negotiation position. Your coach will also help you explore other solutions if you reach a deadlock.

DID YOU KNOW?

You have the choice when it comes to choosing the right family mediator. While your lawyer or your spouse's might recommend someone they know or typically work with, it is by no means a requirement to engage that person. Just like with lawyers, recommendations are a great starting point, however it is important to take the time to "interview" a few family mediators to select the right one for you. What is their area of specialty? How much experience do they have? What format of mediation do they use (online/in person/hybrid/shuttle)? How would they approach helping you sort out the main issue in your divorce? These are all important questions to ask to ensure you are in the right hands for the negotiations ahead.

(3) COLLABORATIVE LAW

This process requires each party to secure their own lawyer to help them lead the negotiations collaboratively through round table meetings. Not all lawyers work as collaborative lawyers; you must ensure you find someone who has that specific training. Typically, once each party has retained a collaborative lawyer, they will all sit down together to try to reach an agreement for the divorce arrangements. This means the parties are supported by professionals who understand the law and will act as third parties to try to unlock disputes. Collaborative lawyers usually charge less than traditional lawyers, so they are often a cheaper option.

In order to begin the collaborative process, each person must sign a Participation Agreement which contains a "disqualification clause". This clause says that if either party commences litigation in court, the collaborative process will end and the current lawyers can no longer represent their clients. In that case, both separating spouses must hire new lawyers and incur further expenses. This was designed as a deterrent to prevent either party from quitting the collaborative divorce process, but it also brings some degree of inconvenience if the process fails.

Just like with mediation, working with a Certified Divorce Coach® in parallel will help you prepare for meetings and clarify your negotiation position.

PODCAST ON COLLABORATIVE LAW

For this episode, I was joined by an expert in this field, Suzanne Kingston. Suzanne is a Solicitor, Collaborative Lawyer and Accredited Mediator and Arbitrator with more than 30 years' experience. She shares her insider view of how collaborative law works in practice and what to expect. Scan the QR code to access the video on You Tube:

The three pre-requisites to using collaborative law are:

1- Signing a Participation Agreement as explained above.

2- Writing an anchor statement that explains why you have chosen Collaborative Law. This statement is referred back to for motivation when the negotiations become too difficult.

3- A true commitment on the part of both spouses to resolving their disputes collaboratively, despite the challenges this path may present.

4 ONE COUPLE, ONE LAWYER

The "One Couple, One Lawyer" model is a growing trend in many countries, such as England & Wales for example. This approach offers a streamlined solution to handling divorces by allowing a single lawyer to represent both parties in an amicable separation. It is intended for couples who are struggling to reach mutual agreements on key issues such as asset division, child arrangements and/or financial support, and who are looking for a legal expert to recommend an appropriate solution. The lawyer's role is to provide neutral legal advice based on what a court of law might rule on the case, thus guiding the couple towards a reasonable agreement. The clients can then choose to endorse the lawyer's recommendations as they stand or to use them as a basis for further negotiations.

One of the primary advantages of this model is its efficiency and cost-effectiveness. By involving just one lawyer, couples can save significantly on legal fees compared to the traditional approach where each spouse hires their own. Many law firms offering these services work on a fixed fee basis, which allows the couple to control costs even further. This model can also reduce the emotional strain and conflict often associated with divorce proceedings, as it encourages co-operation and a joint resolution. For couples who have maintained a civil relationship and can communicate effectively, this can be a less stressful way to finalise their separation.

However, there are some limitations and potential drawbacks to this model. To start with, it is worth checking whether this model is an option in the jurisdiction in which you are divorcing, as it is not allowed everywhere. Second, you should be aware that the drafted divorce agreement is not a legally binding court order, so it still requires both spouses to agree to follow it and to have it approved by a judge. Also, the lawyer must remain neutral and cannot advocate for one party over the other, which can become problematic if a power imbalance exists between the spouses or if one spouse feels pressured into an agreement. Additionally, the "One Couple, One Lawyer" model may not be suitable for cases involving domestic abuse or contested issues, as it requires a high level of trust and cooperation between both parties. Finally, while this option remains a lot cheaper than going to court, it is still more costly than some of the approaches mentioned above.

(5) ARBITRATION

Effectively, arbitration is a private courtroom, with a judge – the arbitrator - whom the couple choose together. It can be leveraged to resolve a variety of divorce disputes[13], from parenting to finances. I have found that it can be particularly useful for a couple who needs help getting past the final roadblocks to finding an agreement. They can then choose to appoint an arbitrator to make a final decision on the issue(s) they can't agree upon.

---

[13] In England & Wales, arbitration could only be leveraged for financial matters until recently, but it has now been extended to cover parenting disputes.

The arbitrator acts as a "private judge" in that the decision they make is final and binding. So, unlike other amicable divorce options, you are still delegating the decision-making to a third party rather than negotiating something acceptable yourselves.

Another thing to note is that arbitration usually costs more than some of the other options outlined here, but it does offer the advantage of having a fixed price. Preparing for the arbitration hearing with a Certified Divorce Coach® will allow you to present credible arguments and a reasonable position, therefore avoiding damaging emotional pitfalls.

PODCAST ON ARBITRATION

To give you a better understanding of what arbitration is and how it works exactly, I invited Rebecca Hawkins to join me on my podcast. Rebecca is a specialist in non-court family problem-solving. She is trained and experienced as an Accredited Mediator, a Family Lawyer, an Arbitrator for Children Matters, a Resolution Trainer and parenting co-ordinator. Scan the QR code to access the video on You Tube:

Rebecca's top three tips to people considering arbitration:

1- Make sure you are specific about the subjects on which you are asking the arbitrator to make a determination.

2- Take time to "shop around" and speak to various arbitrators to find one that you trust.

3- Even if you are self-representing, get some legal advice to ensure you understand the long-term implications of having an arbitrator make a determination.

⑥ NEGOTIATING VIA LAWYERS

This is the least cost-effective of the amicable divorce options but can still lead to a collaborative solution. In this model, each party hires their own lawyer and negotiations begin via the lawyers, typically through an exchange of letters, until an agreement is reached.

Each lawyer is hired to defend their client's specific interests and litigation remains an option if the negotiation fails. Unlike collaborative law, your lawyer will continue to represent you even if you end up going to court. This means it is important that you spend some time understanding your lawyer's philosophy when it comes to divorce: do they tend to be very litigious or more focused on amicable resolution?

Understanding the grounds for divorce

Depending on the country in which you are filing, the grounds on which you can request a divorce will vary. It is therefore important to understand, from the very start, the various grounds for divorce in the country or countries you are thinking of filing in, as this might significantly impact your ability to proceed as you expected.

Mindsets are changing. The initial concept that someone had to be held responsible for the breakdown of a marriage is starting to fade. People are slowly understanding that sometimes things just don't work out. As this cultural shift progresses, judicial systems are increasingly leaning towards the belief that assigning responsibilities in the context of a family breakup isn't helpful. It fosters an atmosphere of finger-pointing and division. This mentality leads to war-mongering and high-conflict divorce.

It was therefore a major victory when England & Wales passed the Divorce, Dissolution and Separation Act in June 2020 (taking effect in April 2022), removing behavioural "facts" for divorce, and allowing couples to proceed simply based on the marriage having irretrievably broken down. This has also meant that couples are no longer divorcing each other but are divorcing on the basis of a common agreement that they no longer wish to stay in the relationship. However, in many countries that allow fault-based divorce, couples have to choose between various grounds for divorce that must be provided in order to proceed. Examples of these include:

- Adultery
- Abuse
- Desertion by the other party
- Separation for more than a certain number of years
- Imprisonment
- Mental illness

The commonly referred to "No-Fault Divorce" law effectively removes the need for specifying any grounds for divorce. Interestingly, in England &

Wales, it also now allows one of the spouses to file for and obtain a divorce without agreement from the other person.

Be aware that not all countries have adopted no-fault divorce laws and clarifying their approach will be essential in making your decision on how to proceed. Many jurisdictions such as Abu Dhabi, Hong Kong or France also offer hybrid options, leaving petitioners the choice between a no-fault or a fault-based approach. Once again, it is always vital to consult a lawyer in the relevant jurisdiction to verify local laws and regulations.

Choosing the right jurisdiction for an international divorce

PODCAST ON CHOOSING THE RIGHT JURISDICTION FOR YOUR DIVORCE

Watch my podcast on choosing the right divorce jurisdiction for more information on what to consider in making this decision. In this episode, I spoke to Lucy Greenwood, Family Solicitor at The International Family Law Group. Scan the QR code to access the video on You Tube:

Lucy's top 3 tips for someone who is considering which jurisdiction to divorce in:

1- Speak to a lawyer in each of the potential countries to see if you can get divorced there and what your legal rights are on divorce.

2. Secure your favoured jurisdiction before suggesting NCDR.

3. Ensure your lawyer has international family law experience.

If you were married abroad, live abroad or are married to someone who does not hold the nationality of your country of residence, you may have a choice of jurisdiction. That is not a decision you want to take lightly.

The first thing you'll want to do is speak to a lawyer in each of the countries you have ties to in order to understand how they compare. For example, prenups and postnups don't have the same value in every country. Similarly, not all jurisdictions have a legal requirement for full financial disclosure during divorce. Also, always consider whether an order made in one country can be enforced against assets located in another. These might end up being important factors in your decision, for example if you are worried about your spouse hiding assets. In that case, a country that mandates a legal documentation of each party's assets might be more favourable to you. But beyond the legal considerations, here are some things you will want to consider when making that decision:

1. Think about the divorce culture. As I have alluded to several times already, different countries have different cultures when it comes to divorce. In England for example, judges are very focused on amicable resolution and strongly encourage couples to go to mediation before hearing their cases. Other countries are much more litigious. So do your research and look back at your divorce goals to make sure that you're choosing the jurisdiction that best aligns with your values and with how you want your divorce to unfold.

2. Look at the costs and build a budget for each jurisdiction. Lawyer and court fees are not the same everywhere. Understand properly what the implications are of each jurisdiction when it comes to these fees.

3. Finally, investigate the divorce laws in each country. Some countries require long waiting periods for example. Several jurisdictions such as Australia, Canada or South and North Carolina in the US require the couple to have been living apart for a year before a divorce can be obtained. Similarly, as mentioned before, some countries don't allow no fault divorce and require a justification for seeking a divorce, called a ground for divorce. Others still require you to have been married a number of years before you can proceed. Finally, certain countries might have specific laws that do not serve you well: in Germany for example, the judge must hear a child if he or she is older than three years, which you may not want to feel obligated to do. So, make sure you understand what those rules are and understand which ones work best for your specific situation.

MISTAKE #3: ANTAGONISING YOUR SPOUSE BY FILING IN YOUR PREFERRED JURISDICTION BEFORE TELLING THEM YOU WANT A DIVORCE

One of the most common issues I see in international divorce cases is the difficult balance between legal protection and values. Many of my clients come to me with the intent of divorcing without going to court, through a negotiated agreement with their spouse. As I will explain later in this book (see Chapter 6 "How do I tell my spouse and children?"), the way in which you initiate the divorce conversation with your spouse is likely to set the tone for the rest of the divorce. An aggressive approach will probably lead your spouse to react defensively, upping the ante and escalating the conflict. A peaceful and respectful conversation is likely to lead to a more controlled response. However, when it comes to securing the best jurisdiction for your divorce, it can be risky to wait too long before filing as it gives the other person more time to act first. This is a dilemma that I see time and again with my clients. Their lawyer usually advises them to file first and without prior notice to their spouse to avoid any jurisdictional conflicts. This is sound advice from a legal strategy perspective. But from a human one?

For those who have a lot at stake by securing one jurisdiction over another, this is a difficult arbitrage. One solution I often explore with my clients is working with their lawyer to gather all the paperwork to file in their preferred country, but to keep their finger over the send button until they have discussed the subject with their spouse.[14] This doesn't mean that you will be informing your spouse of the reasons behind your choice of jurisdiction, it just means that you will have informed them that you are planning to file. While there is still an element of premeditation involved, most people would react less angrily if informed ahead of time by their spouse that they are filing for divorce rather than finding out through correspondence from the court.

If, however, you trust that your spouse has not yet sought legal counsel and/or that they will not react aggressively, the best solution is to inform them of your decision to divorce and work on finding an agreement prior to filing anywhere. The jurisdiction you file in will matter a lot less if you reach a negotiated agreement out of court, as you will not be asking a judge to make decisions for you based on local laws and precedents. However, you might lose bargaining power if the local laws don't align to your interests.

[14] Make sure you discuss this strategy with your lawyer as not all countries allow for electronic filing, which makes it a lot faster to file than in countries that only have paper-based applications.

Chapter 4: How do I get organised?

In a nutshell

1. Gather as much the information and facts upfront as possible.
2. Take the time to build the right divorce team and surround yourself with the right people.
3. Define what success looks like so you know what you are working towards.

Defining the terms of your divorce is probably one of the most important decisions you will be asked to make in your life. The impacts of the agreements you reach will be felt for years to come and will be difficult to amend in the future. If you were applying for a job and had to negotiate your salary, you would certainly take the time to understand what similar roles usually pay, how generous the company's pay packages tend to be compared to their competitors, but also to define the minimum amount you are willing to agree to and what a good salary might look like for you.

Divorce conversations should be approached with the same frame of mind. You will want to take the time to gather information and to define your version of a successful outcome. As with most important events in life, preparation is key. There is no risk and many benefits in being well prepared, and taking the time to do so properly will bring improved results to both parties.

Collecting documents and financial information

Gathering documentation in preparation for a divorce is a critical step that can significantly impact the outcome of the process. It is crucial for ensuring a fair division of assets, accurate calculation of spousal and child support, and protecting oneself against future disputes. This is why, in many countries, both parties will be required to submit some form of financial disclosure information. Here are four primary benefits to gathering this information pre-emptively[15]:

1. It will ensure you are fully prepared once you are asked to share the required documents, taking away some of the stress and overwhelm of doing it ahead of a given deadline (and of having them translated on short notice if need be).

2. It will avoid your soon-to-be-ex providing insufficient information, hiding information or under-evaluating assets during the financial disclosure process. By collecting and organising financial information early on, you can ensure that all income, expenses, assets and debts are accurately accounted for, reducing the likelihood of disagreements during negotiations.

3. Financial documentation is essential for determining spousal and child maintenance. These payments are typically based on income and financial needs, which must be substantiated with evidence. Inaccurate or incomplete information can lead to unfair support arrangements, overburdening one party, leaving the other without sufficient resources, or not providing the children with the resources

[15] This information might need to be updated later on in the proceedings if it has become out of date.

they are due. Having accurate financial records ensures that support payments are fair and reflective of the true financial situation.

4. Gathering financial information helps protect against future legal challenges. Divorce settlements are often final, and any oversights or omissions can be extremely difficult to correct later. By thoroughly documenting your finances, you minimise the risk of future disputes and ensure that the settlement is based on a complete understanding of the financial picture.

Starting this process early is advisable, as it can be time-consuming, particularly if records are scattered across different countries. Systematically collecting and organising documents, both physically and digitally, will streamline the process and reduce stress during a challenging time. I strongly recommend you speak to your lawyer at this stage to understand what financial information you can legally gather without breaking the law with regards to your spouse's data protection rights. Do <u>not</u> send a lawyer anything until you have checked what you can legally share, as inappropriate handling or unsolicited sharing of information can inadvertently lead to them to being removed from your case.

You can find many checklists on the internet, and lawyers often provide similar lists to their clients to help them gather their own documents before kicking off the legal process. In broad terms, the idea is to pull together any information that might be relevant in the future as part of the divorce proceedings. Here is a starting point which you might find helpful to get going, but keep in mind that each country will have its own requirements:

- tax returns from the past five years
- bank statements (ideally 12 months back) from all savings, checking and cryptocurrency accounts, whether local or abroad, even if empty
- property valuations and mortgage statements
- debts: statements for all credit card accounts, personal loan agreements, student loans, real estate and mortgage records...
- pensions information, valuations and statements
- investment account statements
- employment information and income
- other income that you and your spouse might receive: child maintenance payments, government benefits, property rental income...
- household spending budget
- the value of debts that are owed to you
- receipt or valuations of any high value belongings such as jewellery, art, antiques...
- up-to-date statements of any investments
- share valuations
- life insurance policies (including endowments) and surrender valuation for each policy
- list of items in safe deposit boxes or storage
- other insurance policies (health insurance will be particularly important in the United States)
- complete records for any businesses owned
- titles to any vehicles, mileage and condition for all vehicles

Alongside all these documents, you should also locate and review your prenuptial/postnuptial agreement if you have one. While the value of these types of documents varies from one country to the other, it is important to refresh your memory regarding its terms. I would recommend bringing the prenup/postnup to your first meeting with a lawyer to help inform the advice they will give you.

EXPERT TIP

Don't forget to get any documents in a foreign language translated. The requirements for translations to be recognised by the court will vary from one country to the other, so make sure you are getting official and certified copies for the country in which you reside.

Beware: official translations can be costly and take time. I recommend you check with your lawyer to ensure you are having the right documents translated and receive them back in time.

As tedious as it can be, gathering all these documents will ensure you enter the divorce process fully informed and prepared. You will have a full picture of the family finances and a good understanding of what might become part of the division of assets. This will also allow you to make decisions such as how much you want to spend on your divorce and what your strategic priorities will be, based on an informed cost-benefit analysis.

Through the documentation you will have gathered, you will be able to create a list of matrimonial assets to support the financial agreements you will eventually sign. If you aren't sure what is necessary, it is always better to include everything you can think of. Your lawyer can advise later if anything should be excluded from the list. While the list varies from one country to the next, the typical categories of matrimonial assets that might be sold/divided/transferred during divorce include:

- properties (equity only)
- cars, boats, motorcycles
- furniture, antiques, and art
- jewellery
- sports equipment
- businesses (even if owned by only one spouse)
- retirement assets (including pensions)
- savings and bank accounts
- stocks, bonds, VCTs and other investments
- cryptocurrency accounts
- debts owed to you and by you
- cash sums
- air miles

MISTAKE #4: FORGETTING TO UPDATE YOUR WILL AND LIFE INSURANCE

One thing I strongly advise you to do from the very start is to update your Will and Life Insurance policy as soon as you initiate the divorce process. Unless you are comfortable having your soon-to-be-ex inherit your assets if something were to happen to you before the divorce is final, updating these documents early on will ensure your final wishes are aligned with your matrimonial situation.

Keep in mind that in some countries, a 'Will Pending Divorce' is only temporary and will need to be rewritten after the divorce is finalised.

Building the right divorce team

① WHY DIVORCE TAKES A TEAM

One of the most common concerns I hear from my clients relates to financial health during and after divorce. It is not surprising, in this context, that people feel reluctant to hire several professionals to support them during their divorce. The unintended consequence is that they often end up hiring a single professional, often a lawyer, and expect them to provide all the dimensions of support they require. Unfortunately, no single professional can offer this service.

Combining various professionals ensures that all aspects of the divorce are addressed comprehensively. Just like raising a child, divorce takes a village. It is unrealistic to expect one professional to advise on all the aspects and implications of your divorce. I like to share the following comparison with my clients: imagine you required surgery on your back. You would need support from an array of different specialists. The surgeon, of course, but also a nurse and an anaesthetist during the surgery, and a physiotherapist and personal coach to get back into shape afterwards. Divorce is no different. It takes a team of experts to handle all its implications: a coach to help you navigate the process, a lawyer for legal advice, a financial adviser for financial counsel...

I strongly recommend that you bring these professionals together as a coordinated team at key strategic junctions rather than have them work in siloes. This is because legal, financial, and emotional issues are often intertwined, and decisions in one area often impact the others. For example, career decisions made without financial insight could jeopardise your long-term stability.

DID YOU KNOW?

Not all countries require a lawyer to get a divorce. Several jurisdictions allow couples to get a divorce without legal representation by simply submitting their agreement for court approval online. Even when this is possible, I always recommend my clients speak to a lawyer to ensure their draft arrangements are legally robust and include all important elements. The key here is to use your lawyer as a consultant who can advise you on the legal dimensions of your divorce to help you reach solid and future-proof agreements. The lawyer is not there to "defend" you or litigate on your behalf, they are involved because of their extensive knowledge of the law to ensure you are fully informed regarding the legal implications of your decisions.

MISTAKE #5: EXPECTING YOUR LAWYER TO DO IT ALL

One of the mistakes I made early on in my own experience was to expect my lawyer to advise me on all the aspects of my divorce. I must admit, I wasn't even aware of all the other professionals that can offer invaluable support during that time. My divorce team consisted of three people: my lawyer and my parents. It goes without saying that one of the reasons I chose to become a Certified Divorce Coach® is because I wish I had had this type of support myself when I needed it. Another source of advice I would have significantly benefited from would have been a financial adviser. Because I hadn't explored the long-term implications of the financial arrangements I had agreed to, I accepted a proposal which did not account for foreseeable changes to our situation over time. This led to my ex and I having to renegotiate child maintenance payments several times, causing disagreements and unnecessary conflict. Had I taken the time to work with a financial adviser to model my long-term financial health based on the agreements we were discussing, I would have realised that these proposals were not sufficiently fleshed out to remain viable over time.

Below is an exercise that I use with my clients to help ensure that they are getting the right support for the various aspects of their divorce. This is a clean and easy way of identifying gaps or overload on a certain person. I recommend you complete this exercise at the very beginning of your divorce journey.

Think of the star as needing all its arms to fly high in the sky. You need to have someone supporting you with each of the star's arms. On the diagram below, enter the name of a person or category of professional for each arm. One person can fill two roles - but not more than two.

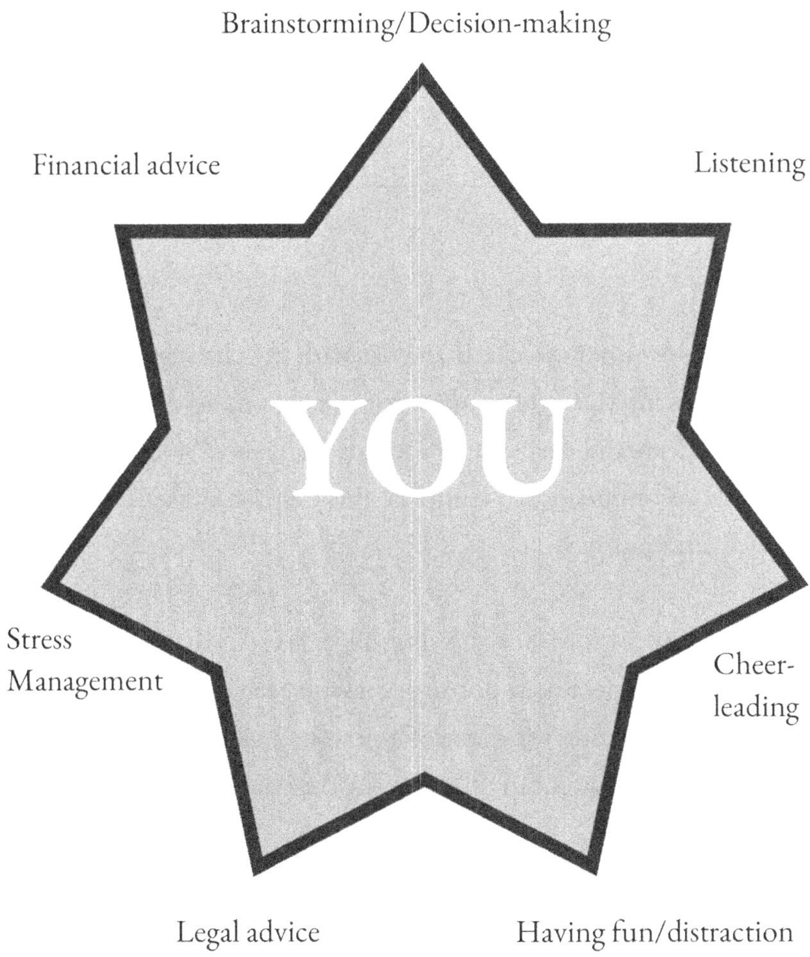
Brainstorming/Decision-making
Financial advice
Listening
YOU
Stress
Management
Cheer-
leading
Legal advice
Having fun/distraction

The table below provides a breakdown of some of the most common professionals that can be called upon during a divorce. This list is far from exhaustive but is designed to give you a high level overview of each professional's role.

THE ROLE OF DIFFERENT DIVORCE PROFESSIONALS

Lawyer	Advises on all legal rights and matters. Negotiates and prepares divorce documentation on client's behalf. Represents client in court, if necessary. Lawyers may be recognised as experts in certain areas of family law, such as high net worth families, international divorce or domestic abuse.
Family mediator	Works with both parties jointly to facilitate the negotiation of the terms of the divorce or separation, ie property division, parenting, etc. Acts as an impartial third party.
Certified Divorce Coach ®	By focusing on their client's future goals and ideal outcomes, a coach helps them to make informed decisions, gain

	clarity, confidence and courage so they can successfully navigate the divorce and its aftermath.
Therapist	Supports the client in examining and understanding what happened in the relationship. Helps client heal from past experiences or trauma. Treats mental health conditions.
Independent financial adviser	Helps evaluate their client's financial situation, including assets, liabilities, and income, and provides advice on the long-term viability of a proposed financial settlement during a divorce. Also assists with post-divorce financial planning, such as setting up new financial arrangements.

② SELECTING THE RIGHT LAWYER FOR YOU

I would like to take a minute here to stress two elements to take into consideration when building your divorce team: which types of professionals you require and who is the best positioned within each professional group to support you. In the work I do with clients who need help with assembling the right divorce team for their situation, I often spend significant amounts of time discussing the choice of their lawyer.

Most of my clients have only two main concerns: how much do they charge and where are they based? While these are undeniably important factors to consider, there are many others that need to be explored before making a decision. Remember, your lawyer will be by your side throughout the divorce process. You need to trust their advice and feel that they understand your priorities and values. So take the time to have a few initial consultations with several potential lawyers, and ask them difficult questions so you can enter this important relationship with the right expectations:

- Do they have experience with your type of situation?
- How much of the work will be done by the partner vs a (cheaper) associate?
- What communication methods will the lawyer use to stay in touch with you and how fast can you expect them to respond?
- Do they know your soon-to-be-ex's lawyer?
- How much money do they estimate you will need to spend based on the complexity of the case?
- How often will you be invoiced and can you get early visibility of legal expenses as they accumulate?
- What is their philosophy with regards to out-of-court dispute resolution options?

These are only a few examples of questions I recommend my clients explore with their prospective lawyers. You can, of course, add or remove any as you see fit. The point here is that you must be sure this is a relationship that is going to work for you, and that you can expect the right support from this person.

If you are getting divorced in a global context, you will want to ensure that the professionals you select have experience and expertise in international divorce. This can be reflected through a number of relevant skills:

- Experience dealing with international divorce cases
- Fluency in your language
- Knowledge and understanding of the family law system in your home country
- Network of professionals who speak your language and who can advise about international divorce challenges (tax advisers, foreign lawyers and mediators, immigration lawyers...)
- Past cases pertaining to the same countries involved in your own divorce

MISTAKE #6: SELECTING YOUR LAWYER BASED ON PRICE

One of my clients came to me after 15 months of divorce conversations with her spouse, realising that her lawyer was not the right person for her. He had been recommended by someone she knew, and she had not spoken to any other lawyers before instructing him. She had been told that he was relatively cheap and that had been enough to make her decision. Fifteen months later, she had spent tens of thousands of pounds in legal fees with a lawyer whom she did not trust and whose advice she did not want to follow. Her divorce had gotten nowhere. One of the first things we did together was to help her properly select a new lawyer. While there is always some additional cost in changing, she eventually found someone who communicated with her much more effectively and who inspired full confidence. The cost saving she thought she was getting by hiring the first lawyer, based on recommendation only, was completely offset by the additional costs and stress this failed relationship led to.

PODCAST ON SELECTING THE RIGHT FAMILY LAWYER

What should you look for in a Family Lawyer when you are going through divorce or separation? What can you expect from their services? What attributes and qualifications matter most? I was joined by Family Solicitor Claire Wood, who kindly answered all these questions for us, and more. Claire is a Legal Director at Kingsley Napley. Scan the QR code to access the video on You Tube:

Claire's three tips to work efficiently with your divorce lawyer:

1- Prepare for the first meeting and come with a list of questions and all the information you have been able to gather to help the lawyer advise you.

2- Be honest with your lawyer, they cannot help you if they don't know the facts.

3- Consider the entire team supporting you, including paralegals, divorce coaches, financial advisers, and therapists.

③ WHO TO LEAN ON FOR EMOTIONAL SUPPORT

According to the Holmes and Rahe Stress Scale,[16] which measures the stress of different life events, divorce is the second most stressful life event after the death of a spouse. Just like bereavement, it marks the end of a significant relationship and can bring a whirlwind of emotions such as sadness, anger, confusion, and even relief. Divorce impacts all dimensions of your life from social circles to professional performance and financial stability. It is no surprise, therefore, that many divorcing individuals find themselves seeking emotional support during this challenging period. Such support can be found in a variety of places, such as friends and family, online communities, professional support and support groups. With each option having its pros and cons, choosing the right type of support based on your needs and budget can make a substantial difference in the healing process.

---

[16] In 1967, psychiatrists Thomas Holmes and Richard Rahe examined the medical records of over 5,000 medical patients as a way to determine whether stressful events might cause illnesses. Patients were asked to rank a list of 43 life events in order of important. Their results were published as the Social Readjustment Rating Scale (SRRS), known more commonly as the Holmes and Rahe Stress Scale.

Friends, family and your faith community

Friends and family are often the first line of support for many going through a divorce. Their familiarity and close connection can provide a comforting presence and a listening ear. They offer unconditional support and can be a reliable source of practical help, such as looking after children or assisting with everyday tasks. However, there are both pros and cons with this line of support.

Pros:

- immediate availability and accessibility
- emotional investment in your wellbeing
- they know you (and your spouse) particularly well and understand your personal situation

Cons:

- emotional bias can sometimes lead to less objective advice, which can be negative and harmful, exacerbating the emotional challenges of divorce
- their advice may sometimes stem from their own experiences rather than from your unique situation
- you may want to keep your divorce private until it is finalised, or simply not put your friends and family in the middle of your disagreements with your ex
- they might be living in another country and therefore be able to offer limited support – this is particularly true in the context of expat divorces, of course.

Social media and online groups

In today's digital age, social media groups dedicated to supporting individuals through divorce are easily accessible. While such groups can offer a sense of community and immediate advice, they should be approached with caution. The unregulated nature of these platforms means that not all advice will be beneficial, and there is a risk of encountering negative or harmful interactions. Privacy concerns are also paramount, as sharing personal details on public or semi-public forums can lead to unintended consequences, such as posts being used against you in court. Furthermore, it is important to note that many jurisdictions have an implied duty of confidentiality in family proceedings, and you must therefore be careful not to share details pertaining to your case online. It is essential to balance social media engagement with more reliable support forms such as professional therapy, coaching or structured support groups led by professionals.

Pros:

- anonymity can encourage openness
- diverse perspectives, insights and experiences
- available 24/7

Cons:

- risk of receiving unqualified or harmful advice from people who do not understand your situation
- potential for exposure to negativity or unhealthy comparisons
- can become echo chambers in which only similar viewpoints are shared, limiting exposure to various perspectives and solutions

- privacy concerns and the potential for personal information to be shared inappropriately, found by your ex or your children, or even used against you as evidence in court.

Therapy and/or divorce coaching

Engaging with a licensed therapist and/or a qualified divorce coach can be one of the most effective ways to navigate the emotional complexities of divorce. For those who don't fully understand the difference between the two, please note that these professions work in different ways: therapy typically focuses on past traumas and experiences, while coaching takes a future and goal-focused approach. Nevertheless, both types of professionals are trained to provide objective, professional guidance and support, helping you process your emotions healthily.

Pros:

- professional, unbiased support
- confidentiality assured
- access to proven therapeutic and skill-building techniques
- divorce coaches can complement other professionals such as lawyers and financial advisers to provide a well-rounded support system.

Cons:

- can be expensive and time-consuming
- may require time to build trust and rapport
- need to ensure you select the right therapist or coach based on your objectives, personal situation and affinities.

Support groups

Support groups, whether in-person or online, offer a structured environment where individuals going through divorce can share their experiences and feelings. These groups are often led by a professional facilitator and provide a balanced mix of peer support and professional guidance from people who understand what you are going through and can share relevant experiences. Support groups particularly stand out for their low-cost, professional, and community-based approach.

Pros:

- safe, structured environment
- often facilitated by professionals
- opportunities to form new friendships and support networks
- access to shared resources and coping strategies
- provide structure and motivate individuals to continue working on their personal growth and recovery
- removes some of the loneliness of divorce in knowing that other people are experiencing or have experienced similar challenges
- low-cost alternative to individual coaching

Cons:

- may require a time commitment
- comfort levels can vary depending on the group's dynamics
- availability might be limited in some areas

Navigating the emotional landscape of divorce is challenging, but with the right support it becomes more manageable. It is therefore important to seek out and utilise appropriate support systems based on the unique benefits they offer. Regardless of the chosen support form, the critical takeaway is that you do not need to go through divorce alone. Seeking support is not a sign of weakness, but an act of strength and self-preservation.

(4) WHAT OTHER PROFESSIONAL SUPPORT MIGHT I REQUIRE?

There are a multitude of other professionals who might come into play during your divorce. These include mortgage brokers, pension specialists, social workers and career coaches among others. I would, however, like to draw your attention to three particularly important matters which I strongly recommend you explore with the appropriate qualified support: tax implications, immigration status changes and pension sharing.

Consulting with a tax adviser

Speaking to a tax adviser early on is indispensable, as tax laws can significantly impact your financial situation and vary widely from one country to another. This is even more important if you have assets in the United States, where taxation is particularly complex. Divorce involves the division of assets, child maintenance and spousal support, all of which have tax consequences that differ depending on local laws. For example, in some countries, child maintenance may be tax-deductible for the payer and taxable for the recipient, while in others, it might not be deductible or taxable at all. Similarly, the division of pensions or real estate could trigger capital gains taxes, which a tax adviser can help you minimise or plan for.

Understanding these nuances is essential to avoid unexpected tax liabilities that could create an imbalance in your divorce settlement. You may be thinking you are trading one property in Germany for another of similar value in Canada, but the changes in ownership might trigger taxes in one country and not the other, meaning they are no longer of equivalent value. A tax adviser can guide you on how to structure your divorce settlement in a tax-efficient manner, ensuring compliance with the law while balancing your financial outcomes. Additionally, they can advise on how the divorce will affect your filing status, potential deductions and tax credits in the years following the separation. Consulting a tax adviser ensures that you are fully informed and prepared, making the division of matrimonial assets smoother and less financially burdensome. This conversation should begin in the preparation phases of the divorce and will continue to be critical as you start shaping your financial settlement.

Checking with an immigration lawyer

One of the most common implications of divorces with an international component, which many people forget to explore, is the impact on immigration status and visa. I have seen many clients, especially since Brexit, realise that their decision to divorce had a direct impact on their and/or their children's ability to remain in the UK. Longer term, it may also affect your ability to visit your children if you are living in different countries. Needless to say, this is not something you want to discover and address in the heat of the moment.

Understanding the immigration implications of divorce - for you and your children - is therefore extremely important, especially for individuals whose residency status is tied to their marriage. Divorce can significantly affect one's right to remain in a country and the consequences can be severe, including potential loss of legal residency, loss of employment, or difficulties in obtaining future immigration benefits. Speaking to an immigration lawyer can provide vital insights and help mitigate these risks.

An immigration lawyer will consider factors such as the type of visa you hold and the length of your marriage to guide you through the necessary steps to protect your rights, such as applying for waivers or transitioning to a different visa category. By seeking legal advice early, you can navigate the complexities of immigration law more effectively, ensuring that your rights and future opportunities are safeguarded.

PODCAST ON IMMIGRATION MATTERS IN DIVORCE

For EU citizens living in England & Wales, I recommend listening to my podcast on "Immigration Matters in Divorce", with Immigration Lawyer Matthew James. Scan the QR code to access the video on You Tube:

Three tips from Matthew:

1- Seek immigration advice early on: for some visas, the event that affects your immigration status is the end of the relationship, not the divorce itself.

2- Consider your children's immigration status and citizenship rights as well; they may have entitlements that require consent from your partner.

3- Your family lawyer may not be able to advise you on immigration issues; be prepared to seek specialist immigration advice.

Reviewing options with a pension on divorce expert (PODE)

As we will discuss in Chapter 5, a financial adviser can provide valuable guidance when making financial decisions during divorce. However, while a financial adviser looks at your finances as a whole, including pensions, a Pensions on Divorce Expert (PODE) is of paramount importance when there are significant retirement accounts to be shared. A PODE will create a comprehensive plan for your financial future focused on pension-specific advice and retirement income planning.

The primary role of a PODE is to help clients understand their options, including contributions, benefits, and tax implications. They can offer advice on managing or consolidating multiple pensions, making decisions on annuities or income drawdown, and maximising retirement savings. They offer two particular services which can prove extremely valuable to avoid making the wrong financial decisions during divorce:

- Valuing pension assets: a pensions adviser helps in accurately assessing the value of pension assets, which can be complex depending on the type of pension. They can ensure you understand the current and projected value of these assets, providing a clear picture of what's at stake.

- Explaining pension sharing options: pensions can be divided in various ways in divorce. In the UK for example, there are essentially three options: pension sharing orders (transferring a portion of one spouse's pension to the other), pension offsetting (trading the value of pensions against other assets), or pension attachment orders (providing a future share of pension income or lump sums). A PODE can explain these options, helping you determine the best approach given your unique circumstances.

The importance of setting clear personal goals and reviewing your values

One of the first things I do with any new client who comes to me in the early stages of their divorce is to set their divorce goals. Divorce goals? They are often surprised: "What's a divorce goal? I didn't realise I had any control over my divorce. I thought it was something that was happening to me, not something I can drive towards a goal". Most people often forget that they are actually 50% of their divorce! As one of the two people in the couple, you are absolutely able to influence the way it is going to unfold and the outcomes you are seeking.

(1) SETTING GOALS FOR THE DIVORCE ITSELF

Independently of how your soon-to-be-ex responds, you have a direct influence on how the divorce process unfolds. I will give you a very simple example: how likely do you think it is you will have an out-of-court divorce if you (1) discuss your decision to divorce with your spouse respectfully and peacefully versus (2) hire a "shark" lawyer and file for divorce behind their back? These are extreme examples, but the point is to show that your actions have consequences. The decisions you make and behaviours you adopt feed into the dynamic of how events unfold. If you think of divorce as a dance, you can choose where to take the next step, no matter where your spouse takes theirs. This does not mean that you have full control over the dance - your spouse can make their own decisions about their next steps too - but it means you are leading your half and not letting the other person be in full control of the choreography. This brings us back to the importance of setting goals and defining your values early on. If your objective is to seek revenge on your cheating spouse, you will not approach things the same way as if your objective is to divorce as cheaply as possible. To help you through this thinking, here are a few questions I find particularly powerful when working with my clients. It is important to be honest with yourself while answering these questions and to be aware that there is no objectively right or wrong answer, just what is right or wrong for you.

- What is your top priority in this divorce (eg limiting costs, limiting stress, moving on quickly, removing your spouse from your life forever, seeking revenge...)?
- What would you like your divorce to look and feel?

- How would you like to feel about yourself when you look back at the way you behaved during that time?
- If your children were to see transcripts of everything that unfolded during the divorce, how would you want them to feel?

Whatever the answer to these questions might be, they will be clear indicators of the best way to proceed, from initiating the process to how you behave throughout. They will also be essential in helping you build your divorce team and in selecting the right professionals for your case, as discussed earlier in this chapter.

(2) SETTING GOALS FOR YOUR LIFE AFTER DIVORCE

By the time the divorce is over, no matter how long and how stressful it turns out to have been, you will be left with a new canvas to rethink your life. Divorce is one of those rare intersections in life when you have the unique opportunity to make radical changes. That might be extremely overwhelming for you, at a time when you are feeling vulnerable and lost. But in many ways, it is an opportunity to reconnect with yourself and what you really want your life to be like. There are very few times in life when you have so many options ahead of you: deciding what to do when you graduate, career change and long-distance relocation are three of the main life crossroads outside of divorce. Whether you have children or not, you now have a lot more freedom to make decisions with regards to your life and to regain some control. Here are some of the questions you might want to reflect on:

- How do I want my life to look and feel when my divorce is finished?
- Who do I want to have as part of my life going forward?
- What do I want to stand for and what are my values?
- Are there any hobbies or other parts of me that have been ignored that I would like to reconnect with?
- Do I want to live in the same house, or do I want to get a fresh start somewhere else?
- What kind of co-parenting relationship do I want to have with my ex afterwards?
- What kind of relationship would I like my children to have with each of their parents?
- Is there anything I would like to change in my professional life?

> "I think about my future. I think about what I want. And I think about it without you."
>
> *Meryl Streep in Kramer vs. Kramer*

Once you have thought through your answers to each of these questions, I suggest creating a visual representation of your objectives through a creative tool that keeps your goals and desires in front of you, as a constant reminder and source of inspiration. Here are three techniques I like to use with my clients, but you are of course welcome to create your own:

- Vision boards: These are a visual representation of your goals, dreams, and aspirations. It's a collage or collection of images, words, and phrases that represent what you want to manifest or achieve in your life.

  Example of a vision board:

- Mind mapping: This is a great technique to organise and visualise your goals and aspirations. Start with a central idea or goal and branch out into related goals, actions, or desires. This helps clarify priorities and create a roadmap for achieving them.

Example of a mind map:

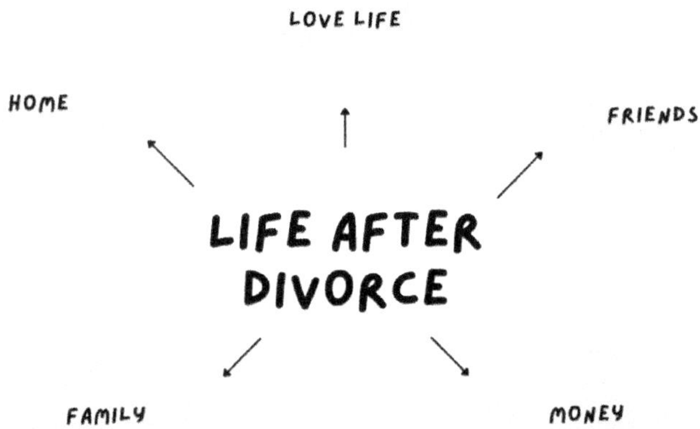

- Future-self journaling: Write letters or journal entries to your future self as if you were already living the life you desire. This can include describing your day, your feelings, and your achievements as if they've already come true, helping you align your actions with your long-term vision.

Documenting your personal objectives from the very start, in whatever form works for you, will help inform your decisions during future negotiations. Indeed, this exercise will have helped you define what is essential to achieve your goals, and what is not. Your personal objectives, combined with your values and your children's best interests, will serve as your North Star and guide you through the many decisions you will be asked to make throughout the divorce.

CONSIDERING RELOCATION TO YOUR HOME COUNTRY AFTER YOUR DIVORCE?

Divorce is a difficult time full of important decisions, especially for those who live abroad. It's quite common for people going through a divorce in this context to consider returning to their home country. It's a natural reflex in times of change and uncertainty: it's tempting to return to a place of comfort, surrounded by family and in a familiar environment. Like a tortoise retreating into its shell when it senses danger, those going through a divorce often feel the urge to seek refuge somewhere peaceful as well. Deciding to return home during a divorce is a highly personal choice, and of course, there's no one-size-fits-all solution. Before speaking to their spouse, those facing this dilemma should take the time to carefully weigh several factors, including the ones below, in order to make the best decision for themselves and their children.

Legal and administrative situation

One of the first things to consider is the legal situation. Has the divorce been granted under the laws of your host country or in your home country? The recognition of the divorce itself, as well as its specific terms, may require additional steps in your country of origin if the divorce was granted abroad. This will be essential if you need to have your divorce agreements enforced in your new country of residence later on – for example, if your spouse stops paying child maintenance. It is important to state upfront that the 1980 Hague Convention specifically forbids one parent from taking the children abroad without the consent of the other. Doing so is a breach of international law and can lead to very serious consequences, including prison.

Children and living arrangements

If you have children, their wellbeing is a top priority. Is stability necessarily the best option for my children or does moving back home present clear advantages, such as being close to extended family or accessing better education?
The spouse wanting to move internationally should spend time with a divorce coach or another qualified professional to prepare a persuasive proposal for their ex-spouse, or for the court, with a detailed plan showing the desire to prioritise the child or children's best interests. Among other things,

considerations include the frequency of visits with the parent remaining abroad, travel expenses to see the other parent, and maintaining each parent's culture and language, if applicable.

Professional situation

Your professional situation is another key factor. Do you have job prospects where you are thinking of going? Do you have transferable skills? Sometimes it's better to remain abroad where your career is established, rather than starting from scratch somewhere else.

Taking the time to fully understand how moving might affect your career prospects, working conditions (such as remote work), and future income will ensure that a return to your country of origin is financially viable for you in both the short and long term.

Emotional and psychological considerations

It's also common for the person making the decision to relocate to view it as a failure. The idea of returning because things didn't go as planned abroad can be hard to accept, even though this is often just a perception in the individual's mind.

It is important to remember that returning home after many years abroad can be challenging. People often feel disconnected from their home culture and are surprised because they thought returning home would be a natural transition.

My advice is to treat a return to your home country as new expatriation, it will likely feel like one.

Financial considerations

Lastly, financial aspects must not be overlooked. The cost of living, taxes, health insurance and school fees are all factors to consider alongside the price of the relocation itself. Creating a comparative budget between the two countries can help clarify your decision. This often highlights costs you may not have thought of, such as travel expenses if the other parent remains abroad or health insurance premiums.

In these budget calculations, you should also take into account the impact a relocation can have on child support payments. In which currency will they be paid? Will the amount change due to the move? Will they suddenly become taxable?

Chapter 5: Can I afford to divorce?

In a nutshell

1. The cost of your divorce is like the length of a piece of string: it depends how you cut it.
2. Budgeting and financial planning for post-divorce life should be among the first things you do.
3. Seek professional support to ensure you aren't making decisions based on emotions only.

When you're considering divorce, one of your most likely concerns is the cost involved. This is completely understandable: divorce can come with a range of expenses, some obvious and others that might take you by surprise. From legal fees and court costs to the division of assets and tax implications, it's natural to feel anxious about how much it will all add up to. The fear of financial strain is one of the main reasons people hesitate to move forward, even when staying in the marriage no longer feels right.

You might also be worrying about the long-term financial impact of divorce. It's not just about paying for the legal process itself; there's the challenge of adjusting to life with a single income, potentially supporting children or maintaining your lifestyle.

That's why it's so important to think through the financial side of divorce before you file. If you start without a clear understanding of the potential costs involved, you could find yourself feeling overwhelmed and unprepared as expenses pile up. You also run the risk of reaching a financial agreement that doesn't meet your long-term needs, leading to frequent renegotiations or requests for variation in court.

So, let's tackle these two aspects, starting with the cost of the divorce itself.

Can I afford to pay for the divorce?

1 PLANNING FOR THE COST OF DIVORCE

One of the first exercises that I encourage my clients to work through is to build a divorce budget. There are, of course, a lot of unknowns regarding costs because the process itself is uncertain. But, through the research you will have conducted, you will have formed an opinion on the type of professionals you will likely be consulting and which divorce route you will likely be taking. When building your budget, ensure you capture all possible costs, not only the legal fees. Some of the costs that people often forget to account for include:

- court application fees for filing for divorce
- in some countries, a barrister to represent you if you go to court (unless you choose to self-represent)
- the cost of the court orders themselves if you are seeking a consent order and/or a child arrangement order
- professional property valuations
- official translation costs for documents in foreign languages

- house moving expenses if you will be moving out of the family home
- an international tax adviser if you have assets abroad.

Use your best judgement to estimate how much you are likely to spend on each element. It can be helpful to determine a maximum sum you are willing to spend for each category or to put checkpoints in place to review expenses and decide whether to change strategies or not. This is something that I find particularly helpful with legal fees. It is quite common for divorcing individuals to be taken by surprise by the speed at which lawyer invoices accumulate. Agreeing early on with your lawyer on a predetermined invoicing schedule can be an efficient way of keeping control of your finances. You can, for example, ask them to invoice you every month, or to invoice you every time they have recorded £1,000 of time on your account. These regular reminders will avoid the unpleasant surprises that usually occur when you receive a bill three months later. They will also allow you to rethink your approach if you find that costs are getting out of hand.

As I mentioned in Chapter 3, there are many different options with regards to how to reach divorce agreements, and they all have various costs associated. One obvious way of limiting your expenses for the divorce itself is to be clear on a strategy and commit to a single avenue for negotiating your divorce agreements. This doesn't mean you cannot pivot if the chosen solution isn't delivering the right results. It means that you have a defined plan for what your next step would be should your first option fail.

In general, it is recommended to start with the cheapest option, ie negotiating directly with your spouse and giving it an honest try. If you understand that negotiations are never straightforward and always lead to some degree of conflict, you will easily understand that it isn't a matter of moving on to the next best option if this approach fails. Decide early on what criteria you will apply to determine whether to keep negotiating directly with your spouse or if it is necessary to bring in third parties such as a family mediator or collaborative lawyers. For example, you can agree with your spouse that if you don't manage to reach an agreement within three months you will go to see a family mediator. This will allow you to take a phased approach to your expenses and make informed decisions about creating new costs for both of you.

MISTAKE #7: CHANGING LAWYERS TOO OFTEN

I have seen many of my clients come to me at a stage where they have already changed lawyers several times, leading to an escalation of costs and disrupting the progress of their case. While it is absolutely right to change lawyers if you feel you are not being represented appropriately, there is a cost associated with this. The new lawyer needs to get up to speed with the case so they will need to spend at least a few hours reviewing all the documentation and speaking to you to understand where you stand. Also, changing lawyers often means shifting strategies. This can sometimes mean that you will have "wasted" money pursuing one divorce route then aborting that approach and moving on to a new idea. This will also have the unfortunate effect of confusing your spouse and their lawyer, probably leading to additional (costly) correspondence to clarify the next steps since the direction of negotiations will have evolved.

As I mentioned in Chapter 4, the key here is to take the time to properly select your lawyer from the start to avoid having to change later on. Should you feel the need to change though, make sure that the costs associated with this pivot are worth the benefits you expect to get.

② OPTIONS FOR FINANCING YOUR DIVORCE

For those concerned about having the funds to finance divorce-related expenses, there are several options to consider. Because the majority of costs usually relate to the provision of legal services, one obvious solution is to try to negotiate a different arrangement with your lawyer. While most of them charge on an hourly rate basis, some lawyers build in some flexibility. For example, you might be able to find lawyers who allow their clients to pay at the end of the proceedings once they have obtained their share of the matrimonial pot. A pre-agreed payment plan or a fixed fee package are also options to explore. It is often difficult to find lawyers who operate on a fixed fee basis in Common Law countries such as the UK and the US because these legal systems are so unpredictable. Be aware also that, in some countries, lawyers charge a success fee based on a certain percentage of the assets you will retain in the divorce or of any spousal maintenance you will receive. Similarly, some lawyers will ask for a retainer, an upfront payment to secure their services, which can be several thousand pounds. It is always worthwhile, however, to have this conversation upfront with your lawyer, and any other divorce professional you hire for that matter, to see how you can manage your cash flow during the divorce itself.

Should this option fail, there are various other avenues you can explore to help bridge your financial gap while you await your financial settlement or payment of your legal costs by your spouse:

Self-financing

- What it entails: Using personal savings or income to cover divorce costs.
- Pros: No need to involve external parties, maintaining privacy and control over finances.
- Cons: May deplete savings or strain current financial resources. May not be financially efficient if that money could be yielding a large interest rate.

Family and friends

- What it entails: Seeking financial support from trusted individuals.
- Pros: Immediate access to funds without the complexities of formal loans.
- Cons: Strains personal relationships, creates potential for conflicts or misunderstandings regarding repayment. In some countries, loans from friends and family aren't regarded as "hard" debt and are treated differently when it comes to the division of assets.

Credit cards

- What it entails: Using credit cards to cover divorce expenses.
- Pros: Quick access to funds, flexibility in repayment.
- Cons: High-interest rates, potential for accumulating debt if not managed carefully. Repayment usually begins immediately.

Personal loans

- What it entails: Borrowing money from a bank or lending institution.
- Pros: Fixed repayment schedule, may offer lower interest rates compared to credit cards.
- Cons: Requires a good credit score, may involve fees and interest charges. Repayment usually begins immediately.

Litigation funding

- What it entails: Obtaining financing specifically for legal fees through litigation funding companies.
- Pros: Covers legal expenses without upfront payment, particularly useful in complex cases. Repayments only begin once divorce is finalised.
- Cons: High interest rates and fees, potential for losing control over legal strategy. Only possible if you have a lawyer.

Legal aid (if eligible)

- What it entails: Government-funded support for individuals who meet specific financial criteria.
- Pros: Provides legal representation at little to no cost.
- Cons: Limited availability and eligibility criteria, may not cover all legal expenses. In England & Wales, Legal Aid does not cover the legal costs of divorce except in some rare cases such as domestic abuse and risk of homelessness. There are some voucher schemes to cover part of the cost of family mediation in some cases.

Remember, each option comes with its own set of advantages and disadvantages. Consider your financial situation, long-term goals, and emotional wellbeing when deciding on the best financing approach for your divorce. Seeking guidance from financial advisers and legal professionals can also provide invaluable support.

PODCAST ON FINANCING YOUR DIVORCE

I recommend you listen to my podcast with Avni Vaghela from Rhea Family Finance. Avni discusses in detail how Litigation Funding works and how much it costs. This is an excellent way of understanding the pros and cons of this financing option. Scan the QR code to access the video on You Tube:

Avni's three tips for those considering Litigation Funding:

1- Speak to the provider yourself and ask all your questions directly.

2- Review the interest rates to ensure you understand how it works.

3- Ensure you have explored all financing options before deciding which is best for you.

Safe money

When going through a divorce, ensuring your financial safety is critical. This is the time to get organised!

First and foremost, it's vital to have access to your own money. Divorce proceedings can take time, and you may need immediate access to funds to cover your living expenses or legal fees. If you don't already have one, open a separate bank account in your name and ensure it's secure and confidential. Check that account contains sufficient money to enable you to live a few weeks at least. Having money that only you can access gives you financial independence and protects you from your spouse suddenly emptying a joint bank account. It also means that your spending will be confidential as your spouse will not have access to your bank statements.

Even if things are starting out amicably, you never know what might happen if your spouse's attitude suddenly changes. For example, I had a client whose spouse was engaging in family mediation with her to reach a financial settlement but who suddenly became extremely upset when he found out she had been seeing someone else since their separation. He became aggressive, thus requiring her to move to a hotel for a few nights until they settled their argument. This is a typical illustration of why it is essential to have access to sufficient funds should anything unpredictable happen.

As I explained in Chapter 4, the divorce process will require you to gather extensive financial information. This means getting hold of details for all your accounts, investments, debts, and assets. By knowing exactly where you stand financially, you can make informed decisions and avoid being caught off guard by any hidden liabilities. If you don't have access to some accounts, speak to your lawyer about how to obtain them without breaking the law. Make copies of all financial documents you can legally access, such as tax returns, pension statements, mortgage details, and bank statements (but, again, check with your lawyer before you do so – privacy laws in England & Wales, for example, include unexpected protections for documents you may think you have a right to see or copy). Such documents will likely be required during settlement discussions. If you suspect your spouse may be hiding assets, you may want to hire a forensic accountant or choose to have your case dealt with in a country where financial disclosure is mandatory. This can help ensure transparency and fairness during the division of assets.

Be proactive in securing your digital finances too. Change all your online banking passwords to prevent any unauthorised access. This might include updating security questions and enabling two-factor authentication for added protection.

You should also safeguard any irreplaceable personal items, such as family heirlooms, jewellery, or other valuable possessions. Consider moving these to a secure location outside your home such as a safe deposit box or a trusted friend's house. As we all know, divorce can sometimes lead to tension, and protecting your personal belongings can prevent them from being used as leverage or, in some cases, from going missing.

Privacy is another area to focus on. If you expect things to get heated, it can be a good idea to open a post office box to receive important mail, such as bank statements, legal correspondence, and pay checks. This ensures your financial information and personal affairs remain private and out of reach of your spouse.

Can I afford to be divorced?

I have yet to meet a single client who doesn't express some form of concern about the impact of divorce on their financial stability. Once again, this is a problem that can be addressed by creating a budgeting spreadsheet. It is a valid concern to wonder how you will cover your living expenses after the divorce, especially if you will be living on a single income. This is especially true for someone who is not used to managing the household finances. One small and easy step that helps address this fear is to put everything on paper. By going through your bank statements, you can create a budgeting spreadsheet with estimates of your expenses after the divorce. This will allow you to visualise what you will need to sustain yourself if you want to keep the same lifestyle and can continue to be of use as you manage your household budget independently after divorce. If, even after taking into account potential spousal and child maintenance, the numbers don't add up, this will be an opportunity to review and reprioritise your expenses to achieve a positive balance. Some of these decisions might be very difficult to make, but you are better off being aware of them early on rather than living above your means for several months before realising you have accumulated a huge debt or overdraft.

1 WORKING WITH A FINANCIAL ADVISER DURING DIVORCE

Divorce in most jurisdictions involves splitting assets, pensions, properties, and even liabilities such as debts. A financial adviser with experience in divorce can help you understand your financial landscape and plan accordingly. They can also model different scenarios so you can test the financial impact of various settlement options.

TYPICAL QUESTIONS TO BRING UP WITH YOUR FINANCIAL ADVISER

- Will I be able to maintain my current lifestyle after divorce?

- Is this a good agreement for my retirement?

- Does this proposal provide me with the right mix of assets and ensure I have enough liquidity?

- Am I taking on debt?

- Can you help me manage my investments?

- How will the terms of the agreement impact my taxes?

Benefits of using a financial adviser in divorce

There are many reasons why I recommend my clients consult a financial adviser:

1. Objective financial assessment: Divorce can cloud judgement, leading to emotional decisions that are not always financially sound. A financial adviser provides an objective perspective, ensuring that you approach financial matters logically rather than emotionally. The hard facts you gather from your conversations with a financial adviser will then find their way back into your divorce coaching sessions as some of the elements to consider in your decision-making.

2. Tax efficiency: Without proper advice, many people overlook the tax implications of asset transfers. A financial adviser can guide you in structuring the division of assets to minimise tax burdens, ensuring you don't lose a significant portion of your assets to tax bills. This is particularly important in international divorce, when there are assets in various countries and you will need a specialised professional to advise on the different tax regimes and implications (see Chapter 4 for the role of tax advisers in divorce).

3. Pension division: Pensions are often one of the largest assets to be divided in a divorce. They can be complex to assess and divide, especially if one party has a defined benefit pension or is a higher earner. While you may choose to consult a pensions specialist,[17] your financial adviser will consider your pension as part of an overall financial strategy, as one of the pieces of the larger financial puzzle they address. They can also advise you on various options such as pension sharing, pension offsetting or pension attachment.

4. Planning for the future: Post-divorce, your financial needs and goals may change significantly. A financial adviser helps you create a tailored financial plan to safeguard your future, including retirement planning, education funding for children, and even advice on how to invest a settlement wisely. For those who are less financially savvy or aren't used to managing the family's finances, this will be a

---

[17] See Chapter 4 for information on the role of a Pensions on Divorce Expert.

unique opportunity to learn the basics and ensure you are in control of your financial health going forward.

5. Avoiding costly mistakes: Many individuals underestimate their long-term financial needs post-divorce or mismanage settlements. A financial adviser can help ensure that decisions made today will provide financial security for years to come. By modelling your proposed settlement agreement and alternative options, you will build a very clear picture of the financial sustainability of these proposals, which will help you with decision-making and negotiations.

When to bring a financial adviser on board

The best time to involve a financial adviser is at the beginning of your divorce process, alongside your divorce coach and your lawyer. Early involvement ensures they have a full picture of your financial circumstances and can work with your legal team to achieve a fair and sustainable settlement.

Financial advisers are also extremely helpful during mediation or negotiation phases, working behind the scenes to evaluate offers and counter-offers, providing clear advice on whether a settlement is in your best financial interest.

CASE STUDY: AVOIDING PENSION PITFALLS

One of my clients, a middle-aged teacher, assumed her husband's pension was worth less than the family home and agreed to keep the house in exchange for waiving her claim to the pension. Her financial adviser showed her that his defined benefit pension was worth considerably more. This information proved extremely valuable in our coaching sessions as it allowed us to think of alternative proposals to discuss with her husband. I coached her on how to discuss this new information with him and she managed to negotiate a more balanced settlement that included both pension sharing and property rights.

② CAN I AFFORD TO KEEP THE FAMILY HOME?

One of the most common concerns I hear from my clients is whether they can afford to stay in the matrimonial home. Along with retirement savings, the family's main residence is often one of the most contentious marital assets during divorce. This is partly because it is usually the highest valued asset a family possesses,[18] but also because of the sentimental value that is attached to it. Many homes are full of memories and childhood tokens that can be very comforting at a time of major change. It is quite common in this context for one or both of the parents to make remaining in the house one of their priorities when negotiating the divorce settlement. Because there is no steadfast rule with regards to who keeps the family house, this emotional attachment becomes a major factor in determining the financial arrangements, sometimes to the detriment of other financial assets that could be obtained.

There are many elements you will need to consider when deciding whether keeping the house at all costs is the best approach. Each situation will be different, and every individual's decision will be based on their own set of circumstances. But it is important to ensure that all the implications of the decision have been weighed from the start.

The advantages of keeping the family home

The most common driver behind the objective of keeping the family home relates to the stability of the children. At a time when everything is changing and uncertainty reigns, as a parent you probably seek to preserve as much familiarity as possible in your children's lives. It is true that they are absorbing a large amount of volatility and that keeping some

[18] The average UK house price was £285,000 in March 2023.

things steady often helps with the transition. Your children may have never lived in another house or known another bedroom. If they are very young, this will probably have less meaning. However, teenagers might feel particularly attached to this familiar space. Furthermore, moving houses can often require changing schools, which creates yet more turmoil for the children, ripping them away from their habitual social circle and environment at a time when they are already having to settle into a new reality.

The other advantage of staying in the family home is the fact that it removes yet another source of stress in your life: that of finding a new home, arranging a move and settling into a new residence. There are already so many things to deal with during a divorce, and the experience is often so challenging, that the last thing you want is yet another difficult change to manage. Staying in the family home will give you something steady to hang on to while your world is being turned upside down.

Last but not least, depending on the family's involvement in the local community, moving houses can lead to a breaking of community bonds which are particularly important during a divorce. Having your friends and family nearby, knowing your neighbours and your local shop keepers are all welcome elements of comfort during this life transition.

The challenges of staying in the family home

There is an obvious financial implication linked to keeping the family home as a single income household. If you are the parent who is hoping to stay in the house, you should always do some proper budgeting before making the decision, to ensure you can afford to pay the mortgage (or rent) and maintain the house on your own. A thorough understanding of all costs and expenses relating to the house, on a monthly basis, will allow you to gain clarity as to whether the numbers add up in your favour or not. You may decide to sacrifice other expenses to make your budget work, but this needs to be carefully considered to ensure it provides a viable setup. The downside of keeping the family home can be that you find yourself cash poor, owning a nice property but not being able to afford anything else, including things that contribute to your personal wellbeing such as holidays, hobbies and restaurants. It may also mean that you must take on new responsibilities that you are not used to shouldering on your own: dealing with roof leaks, renewing home insurance or managing mortgage payments are some typical examples. While all of these are skills that can be acquired over time, they do add to the mental load and expenses of maintaining a family residence.

On the other hand, leaving the past behind and starting afresh in a new home may offer some advantages. It creates a distinct "before and after" break point and can help with emotional healing and recovery. Sometimes, staying in a house full of memories, acquired at a time when you thought you would be living happily-ever-after with your spouse, can create a recurring heartbreak and prevent you from moving on. A fresh start in a new residence that has been chosen and decorated without the involvement of your ex creates a better context for a new beginning. If you are the one staying in the home but are struggling to accept the divorce or still grieving the relationship, a move to a new residence might be worth considering for your mental wellbeing.

MISTAKE #8: FOCUSING ON EMOTIONS RATHER THAN NUMBERS

Given the pros and cons mentioned above, it is not uncommon for divorcing individuals to make the wrong decision with regards to the family home. This is yet another example where letting your emotions dictate your decisions can be dangerous and unwise. When emotions run high, intelligence often runs low. To avoid this pitfall, the decision needs to be approached as a business transaction, considering the financial and logistical implications of moving vs staying. One of the most common errors that you might make due to your emotional attachment to the family residence is that you are setting yourself up for significant financial challenges in the future. If you are truly willing to give up everything else to keep the house, you may end up foregoing important sources of income in later life, such as pension shares. This might be an acceptable decision if you are still young or have a large pension of your own, but such a decision should definitely be explored in depth with the support of a financial adviser. The priority here will be to avoid ending up strapped for cash during retirement. Predictable variations in the value of the property should also be considered as well as how much mortgage remains to be paid.

Options for dealing with the family home during divorce

As I stressed above, what you and your spouse choose to do with your home will have a significant impact on your future financial health, so it is important to think carefully about the best options for you in the long term. Rules may vary depending on the country, and the tax implications of one solution vs another can be significant. It is worth seeking advice to fully understand the implications, including taxes, of each of the options before making any firm decision. In many countries, such as England & Wales, there are essentially three options with regards to dealing with the mortgage after divorce:

Option 1: Keep the house and mortgage in joint names until an agreed date or trigger event. This approach maintains a financial link between the couple, which can last for many years after the divorce. There are two main cases when this can be a useful solution:

- If one of the spouses cannot afford to buy the other one out and remortgage on their own.[19] One solution in this case is for the person who wants to stay in the family home to pay rent to the other person until they are able to buy them out or to move out. There are many creative options that can be used to help make this arrangement, depending on the country.

---

[19] This arrangement is called a Mesher Order in England & Wales.

- When the parents want to let the children stay in the family home until they reach a set age and agree to take turns living in the house with the children. This is commonly referred to as "nesting". In this case, the parents alternate living in the family home with their children until a pre-determined trigger event or a specific date. At that stage, the property will be sold and the proceeds shared according to a pre-agreed arrangement. Of course, this requires the parents to have another place to live when they are not with the children in the family home.

Option 2: Sell the house and divide any equity. In this case, the couple pays off the mortgage after the sale of the house, then shares the remaining equity. The negotiation is focused on how to share this equity in the context of their overall financial settlement.

Option 3: One party buys out the other's interest in the house and takes on the mortgage in their sole name. This requires checking that the spouse buying out the other can afford to take on the mortgage on their own as well as meet the mortgage payments and maintenance costs going forward. They may pay the other spouse in cash for their share of the remaining equity or offset the value of their share against other assets. If the property is abroad, make sure you are clear about who bears the risk of the variations in exchange rates, especially if you are buying out your ex and offsetting the house against other assets.

As we've just seen, the question of the family property can be a particularly tricky one. Each person will have to weigh the pros and cons of staying or leaving based on their specific set of circumstances and financial ability to stay. There is really no right or wrong answer in this matter, it all comes down to having fully considered all the implications of one decision or the other. My main piece of advice for this is to try to approach the situation in an objective and factual way, to avoid creating a financially unsustainable future.

Supporting yourself after divorce

One of the most common mistakes people make post-divorce is assuming that their expenses will be drastically lower than before. In reality, even if you're downsizing or adjusting your lifestyle, only some costs will be reduced, such as food shopping perhaps. But most expenses remain the same, and some new ones, such as child support or childcare, may appear. It is crucial to review your past bank statements to get a clear picture of what you're really spending now. Look at both regular expenses and non-routine ones—such as travel, medical expenses, and home maintenance—and make sure you adapt these figures based on your expected post-divorce living situation.

One major expense many parents overlook is school-related costs. Parents in the UK spend an average of £6,000 per child on essentials like school uniforms, lunches, trips, and equipment during primary school alone![20] If your child attends a private or fee-paying international school, these costs can escalate even more, so don't forget to budget for your share of school expenses as well. Even small amounts such as paying for school uniforms or new shoes every year add up quickly, so be realistic about what you will need to cover in the future.

If you weren't the one handling household finances during the marriage, the thought of managing a budget may seem daunting. However, it's not as difficult as it might first appear; it simply requires some organisation. Start by listing your income, regular bills, and any new or expected changes in your finances. Don't forget to include non-routine costs, such as passport renewals, car servicing, or holiday travel, as these can significantly affect your budget if unaccounted for. When in doubt, it is always better to over-estimate amounts than to downplay them: you'd rather have some money left at the end of the month than be in the red! In the same spirit, I strongly recommend creating a small pot for "miscellaneous spending" to cover all the ad hoc expenses that you will have outside of your usual budget (parking tickets for example or buying a new toaster).

If you're unsure where to start, consider seeking help. Divorce coaches are specifically trained to help you develop a divorce and post-divorce budget. Additionally, taking a short class or workshop on money management can boost your confidence and give you the tools you need to stay on track.

---

[20] According to the National Foundation for Education Research.

Budgeting for life after divorce is about facing the realities of your new financial situation and planning accordingly. With a bit of effort and the right support, you can build a budget that gives you peace of mind and a solid foundation for the future.

EXPERT TIP

Don't forget about debts! Managing debts after a divorce requires a strategic approach to prevent further financial strain. First, it's important to assess and organise all debts to understand the interest rates, repayment terms, and balances of each account. Consider consolidating multiple debts into a single loan with a lower interest rate to simplify payments and reduce the overall cost. If managing debts becomes overwhelming, seeking help from a professional debt support agency can provide guidance on negotiating better terms with creditors or even debt restructuring. This can help prevent falling behind on payments, which could affect both spouses' credit scores and complicate the divorce settlement. It's crucial to address these debts early, as unresolved financial obligations can lead to lingering issues long after the divorce is finalised.

PODCAST ON TIPS AND TRICKS FOR MANAGING YOUR MONEY AFTER DIVORCE

For this episode, I was joined by Laura Tynan, aka The Witch of Wall Street, Financial Educator for Women. Laura answered my questions about the financial impact of divorce on women and some of the tools and strategies they can leverage to empower themselves financially during and after divorce. Scan the QR code to access the video on You Tube:

Laura's three tips for women who want to become confident in their relationship to money:

1- Get personal with your finances: know what you have and review it regularly.

2- Take time to understand the different ways in which you can build wealth.

3- Come in with the right mindset: success is 20% strategy and 80% psychology.

Chapter 6: How do I tell my spouse and children?

In a nutshell

1. Practice and prepare these important conversations.
2. Reassure your children and keep them neutral.
3. Keep it as peaceful as possible: what you say and do matters.

Sharing the prospect of a separation or divorce with your spouse and children is never an easy task. The thought of explaining your decision while also managing your own emotions can be overwhelming. I have spent countless hours with clients preparing for these conversations and ensuring they didn't trigger a conflictual reaction. I am a strong believer that with careful planning and preparation, you can make this difficult conversation more manageable. Taking the time to think things through beforehand will help ensure that the discussion is as calm and constructive as possible.

Throughout this chapter, I will share my tips for preparing for these two particularly difficult conversations – ie with your spouse and with your children. They centre around four key priorities:

- managing your own emotions
- choosing the right moment and setting
- planning and practicing what you are going to say
- preparing for different reactions

Telling your spouse you want a divorce

This is by far one of the most difficult conversations you are likely to have in your life. Not only are you formalising a monumental decision, you are telling someone you once loved that you no longer believe in your "happily ever after". The manner in which you choose to begin the divorce sets the tone for the entire process and for your relationship with your ex afterwards. Some people opt for an aggressive approach, filing for divorce without informing their spouse and creating an element of surprise. Others choose to begin their post-marriage story with a collaborative and respectful approach. Unless they are in an extreme situation, such as domestic abuse, I always encourage my clients to have an honest conversation with their spouse.

Most of us have close friends or family in which we confide and who help us in making the decision to end our marriage. Aside from this small group of confidantes, it is important to prioritise discussing the subject with your spouse before informing people around you, and definitely before speaking to your children. I once had a client come see me because he was desperately trying to get his wife to speak to him again after she found out that he had already told all their friends that he was leaving her, before even informing her of his decision. Needless to say that if you are trying to preserve a respectful relationship with your soon-to-be-ex, you should communicate your decision in the order outlined below: your spouse, then your children, and finally your wider social circle.

Throughout the divorce, there will be many conversations with your spouse on what happens next. However, before diving into any negotiation about the terms of your divorce, I encourage you to complete two very important initial steps:

- preparing yourself for the conversation
- encouraging your spouse to pursue a low-conflict resolution.

(1) PREPARING FOR "THE CONVERSATION"

Think back to some of the most important conversations you've had in your life. How many have there been? For most people, the answer is just a handful. There is no doubt that the conversation you have with your spouse, informing them that you want a divorce, will make it to the list as well. My recommended approach to "having the conversation" revolves around three pillars which conveniently spell out "GPS".

G for "Gain clarity on your objectives"

As I have mentioned several times in this book, it is important to take time up front to educate yourself about divorce. And that is what you are doing by reading this book.

Before speaking to your spouse, I encourage you to set a clear intention for the conversation. Divorce should never be used as an idle threat nor is it the right solution if both spouses are willing to work on improving their relationship. Ask yourself: are you truly asking for a divorce or simply trying to ring an alarm bell to get your spouse to attend couples counselling with you? Are you suggesting you first try to separate before making a decision, or do you want to get divorced as soon as possible? Whatever your objective, be sure you are clear about it, and you are truly committed to it.

P for "Prepare what you're going to say"

If you are having this conversation, it probably means that you have a degree of respect for your spouse. It is important to have empathy too. Alongside practicing the message you want to deliver, it can help to prepare for various potential reactions from your spouse and to have a defined course of action for each scenario. Role-playing and scripting what you are going to say ahead of time can be useful tools to explore with your divorce coach when preparing for this.

The other advantage of practicing what you are going to say is that it helps you stay focused on the business at hand and allows you to take a step back from your emotions. This means you are less likely to experience very strong reactions when you are speaking and are more likely to keep your composure. If, however, you feel at any point during the conversation that you are being overtaken by emotions (grief, anger, frustration...), keep in mind that it is better to stop the conversation and finish it at a later time than to continue down the path of an emotional confrontation.

One of the fundamental elements here is to make the conversation constructive. Remember that this is a forward-looking conversation, not an opportunity to assign blame or revisit past feuds. The objective here is not to have another argument but to leave the past behind you and start thinking about how to create separate futures in a non-destructive way.

At this point, you may already want to start thinking about your expectations regarding the way you want your separation to unfold. How soon do you want to file for divorce? Will you continue to cohabit during the divorce or live in separate houses? Do you want to try to resolve things together informally or do you need legal advice? How do you envisage your relationship post-divorce? These are important questions to ask yourself before speaking to your spouse, as they will help you paint a realistic picture of how you see things progressing should they ask you. The overall message you want to convey in this first stage is that you would like to keep things amicable and work together through this transition without letting your disagreements turn into a war. The objective of this conversation is to inform your spouse of your decision and set the stage for a co-operative divorce resolution, not to agree to the terms of the divorce there and then.

THINGS TO THINK ABOUT AHEAD OF THE CONVERSATION

How will you manage the question WHY? This is likely to be the first question to come out of your spouse's mouth, so take time to prepare how you are going to explain your decision. Once again, this isn't about assigning blame or convincing the other. Try to articulate your "why" around the situation you are in today rather than past events. For example "I am unhappy in this marriage and I need a fresh start" or "We seem to have forgotten how to make each other happy". Ensure your answer includes how you might have contributed to the end of the marriage too.

What will your spouse's main concern be? State that concern upfront to show that you understand what they care about. For example: "I know you will be worried about how the children (or your parents) will react".

Consider elements you can both agree on. How can you explain your decision based on undeniable facts? For example, "We have been growing apart over the past several years".

Define what is it you are striving towards: Explain your intention clearly and what you expect to come from this conversation. For example: "I would like us to find a respectful and peaceful way of separating that doesn't involve a horrible legal battle".

What positives can you include? Make sure you take time to acknowledge what was good in the relationship and some of your spouse's qualities. There is nothing more heart-breaking than hearing that your marriage has been horrible from start to finish. This is rarely the case and telling yourself and your spouse that narrative can only make it harder to move on with confidence after the divorce.

Acknowledge challenges: Think of any cultural expectations your spouse might be concerned about or significant challenges that they might already be facing that will make this situation harder. For example, if they come from a very religious background and will likely receive disapproval from their family for getting divorced.

S is for "Setting yourself up for success"

Thinking through the actual setting for the conversation can help provide a sense of control and avoid mishaps. You will want to consider three elements: the form, the time and the place.

• The form: I always recommend having these conversations face to face as this type of announcement requires some personal contact. Avoid emails or text messages in particular, as they do not allow you to hear the other person's tone of voice and can often be misinterpreted.

• The place: Choose a place that is neutral, safe and allows you to have a potentially emotional conversation without interruption. If you feel safe doing so,[21] your house is a logical setting to have the conversation as you will both be more relaxed than in a public space.

• The time: It may seem obvious, but it is always better to have this conversation at a time when there is no live argument between you and your spouse. This needs to be a calm and rational conversation and it cannot be managed properly when emotions are already riding high. If you have children, it is important to choose a time when they are not in the house nor likely to return unexpectedly. It is very difficult to predict how long the conversation will last and how your spouse will react. You would not want your children overhearing your exchanges or walking in halfway through.

MISTAKE #9: FORGETTING ABOUT YOUR PERSONAL SAFETY

I have already mentioned the need to protect yourself financially and technologically. Before having the conversation with your spouse, take some time to consider your personal safety. Revisit any patterns exhibited by your spouse in past stressful situations. How do they typically react? What might that require you to do? If you are concerned about your

[21] See Mistake #9 in the next box for more on safety.

personal safety during this conversation, you may want to talk to them in front of a neutral third party, such as a therapist, or you may want to conduct the conversation in a public place.

As I mentioned in Chapter 5, with the example of my client whose husband's anger led her to stay in a hotel for a few nights, make sure you have a safe place to go if the conversation gets out of hand (and money to pay for it!). You may want to inform a close friend or family member about the conversation ahead of time so they can check up on you afterwards. You should also ensure that any tracking apps on your phone are disabled and that you change all your passwords on email accounts, bank accounts and your phone. Finally, set up a new email address, which your spouse will not know about, to use exclusively for the purposes of communicating with your divorce team. Do NOT use your work email as you may need to refer back to these communications for many years to come, and those emails will be lost if you change jobs.

No matter what, remember that you can't control your spouse's reaction to the news, but there are ways that you can reduce the anger and encourage understanding.

② ENCOURAGING YOUR SPOUSE TO PURSUE AN AMICABLE RESOLUTION

Once you have spoken to your spouse about your decision and given them time to take in the news, you can begin the gentle art of encouraging them to do things in a low-conflict manner. This conversation might occur as a logical continuation of the initial announcement discussed above but be aware it might take a few days or weeks for your spouse to be ready to discuss the practicalities of your divorce. Remember that while you may have been thinking and planning for divorce for months (or years!), your spouse may not be in the same place as you at all. I have had many clients over the years who have felt unable to proceed with divorce negotiations because they needed more time to absorb the news of their spouse's decision to end the marriage. Comments such as "I don't want to talk about it, he/she is going to change his/her mind" or "If we just take a little break, it will all get better" are natural reactions when you've just found out that life as you know it is ending. In the cycle of grief, people are still stuck in the denial or bargaining stages while their spouse is already fully accepting the situation.

It is therefore best not to rush into having this conversation if your spouse is showing signs that they are still having trouble processing the news. You also want to avoid giving the impression that you have the road ahead all figured out, as that will likely make them feel betrayed and defensive. However, I would also recommend not waiting more than a few weeks, as you want to speak to them before they potentially seek advice from professionals and friends who might encourage a more belligerent approach.

First and foremost, remember that your own behaviour will set the tone for your relationship going forward. Try to continue to act respectfully and to have regular conversations as things evolve. Beyond leading by example, there are several things you can do to help encourage a low-conflict approach to your divorce.

> "It's not about winning or losing; it's about finding a way to let go, and to be okay. The legal stuff will sort itself out, but the pain of it all is in the way we choose to deal with it, together."
>
> *"The Story of Us" by Dani Atkins*

Sharing resources to encourage a co-operative approach

After you've initiated the discussion, it's important to introduce the idea of handling the divorce co-operatively. You can help your spouse understand that there are alternative ways to manage the separation without resorting to litigation. Tell them about the various NCDR options we discussed in Chapter 3 and highlight the pros and cons of each. You might find it easier to simply share resources with them that explain mediation or collaborative law—without overwhelming them with too much information—to help them see the benefits of non-adversarial approaches. You could also encourage your spouse to consult with a mediator or collaboratively trained lawyer to discuss how these approaches might work. You will be the best judge of what approach they might be most responsive to. But remember to introduce these ideas calmly. The goal is to show them that a co-operative, solution-focused mindset can lead to fairer outcomes and lower stress for both parties by avoiding destructive legal battles.

Maintaining ongoing communication

An essential part of keeping the divorce amicable is establishing a framework for ongoing communication. Divorce is an evolving process, and things can quickly become heated if there's a lack of dialogue. After that initial conversation, you should consider setting up regular check-ins with your spouse to discuss the progress of the separation, how your children are coping and outstanding decisions to be made. These touchpoints can help keep both of you engaged and reduce the risk of misunderstandings or frustrations festering over time.

These regular conversations can be about practical matters such as financial arrangements, property division, or child arrangements, but they can also include emotional check-ins. Allowing space to discuss how each of you is coping can strengthen the bond of co-operation and demonstrate that you're both working towards a resolution that respects both sides.

While transparency is important, it's equally vital to be mindful of boundaries. Divorce is an emotional time and setting limits on how and when certain topics are discussed can protect both of you from feeling overwhelmed. For example, you could agree that certain sensitive matters, such as financial settlements, are only discussed during mediation sessions or specific check-ins. This structure helps prevent heated arguments from derailing the process and allows both parties to remain focused on the bigger picture.

Building a supportive professional team

The professionals you involve in your divorce can make a significant difference in keeping things amicable. Beyond choosing lawyers or divorce coaches committed to a co-operative process, it's important to consider involving other experts, such as family mediators or therapists, who can support the practical and emotional aspects of the separation. As we discussed in Chapter 4, having a trusted team that prioritises amicable resolutions can ease the pressure and provide clarity, allowing you and your spouse to focus on working together rather than against each other.

One way to guide your spouse towards a more amicable resolution is by suggesting professional networks that focus on co-operation. Organisations such as *Resolution*, an England & Wales-based group of lawyers and professionals committed to constructive family law, can be helpful. In the US and the UK, the *Amicable Divorce Network* provides a directory of all types of divorce-related professionals focused on out-of-court dispute resolution. In France, the organisation *Les Avocats de la Paix* was developed with the same purpose in mind. Whatever the relevant organisation in your country, it is worth exploring who they are and how they can help. The aim is to connect your spouse with professionals who are dedicated to fostering communication and resolving issues without confrontation.

Focusing on the bigger picture

Regularly reminding yourself of the larger goals—such as maintaining a respectful co-parenting relationship, achieving financial stability, or ensuring the wellbeing of your children—can help de-escalate potential conflicts.

Whenever tensions arise, shifting the focus back to these broader objectives can help defuse disagreements before they spiral into major disputes. A co-operative mindset, paired with a focus on long-term goals, often leads to more sustainable and amicable outcomes. Encouraging your spouse to see the value in this approach can help them realise that working together is mutually beneficial.

EXPERT TIP

I would strongly recommend you start keeping a journal of events from the day you first speak to your spouse about a possible divorce. The sooner you can start, the easier it will be to keep these records up to date as things evolve. Make sure you keep this physical or digital document in a safe place, out of reach of anyone else, especially your spouse and children.

Here are a few reasons why documenting a chronology of events might come in useful:

- Remembering what happened when: your divorce will, at the minimum, last several months. Even if everything moves ahead swiftly, you will need to share details of events with your lawyer as the context for your case. In the unfortunate event where things don't go as smoothly as you hoped, you will have easy access to a detailed timeline of everything that happened and any supporting documentation. Make sure you include how you were feeling at the time of each event you record and note down as much detail as possible in case things get confusing later on.

- Helping you visualise progress and key turning points: keeping a journal will also be a great way for you to keep a close eye on how the divorce is progressing. By documenting key dates, agreements, and turning points, you can better visualise the progress of your case and identify patterns or delays. For example, you may notice that you and your spouse always get into arguments the day before family mediation meetings. Seeing this pattern on paper will allow you to break this cycle proactively going forward.

- Clarity and Focus: Writing things down helps you process complex situations more clearly, reducing the risk of forgetting important details or feeling overwhelmed by the process. Seeing how far you've come can also boost confidence and provide a sense of accomplishment during a challenging time.

There are apps available online, such as My Case[22], that allow you to record events in a highly visual manner and share this electronically with your divorce team. Or you can simply pick up a notebook and document your journey manually. Whatever works best for you is fine, the key is to keep this information up to date and as thorough as possible.

Does this feel like overkill? Keep in mind that it is a very low effort to keep these records, and that if all goes well you will be able to dispose of them soon. If things don't go according to plan, the last thing you will want is to add to your worries by having to rebuild a timeline of events weeks and months after they've occurred.

[22] www.mycase.com

Telling your children

Telling your children about your divorce is of course one of the most difficult conversations you will have as a parent. Many of the principles outlined above will apply here as well.

As parents, you will want to give some thought to the context in which you will share the news. What is the best time of day for your children? Is it best to tell them all at once or individually? Where is a good place to discuss this? The same considerations about practicing what you are going to say and preparing for various possible reactions apply as well. Keep in mind that your children might need time to process what you have just shared and might not have any questions to ask at that exact moment.

Because every family is different, there is no steadfast rulebook with regards to how you handle this conversation. Here are, however, some key considerations that can guide you through this delicate discussion. After sharing these overall considerations, I will provide some practical tips for telling your children, based on their age group.

① WHEN TO TELL YOUR CHILDREN

Deciding on the right time to tell your children about your divorce is key. Ideally, you and your spouse should tell them together, when you are both ready to provide some concrete details. The conversation should take place once the decision to divorce is final, and not when you are still contemplating it. Children need to feel that their parents are united and providing them with certainty helps reduce feelings of anxiety and confusion.

The best time to tell your children is when you can dedicate the necessary time and attention to their immediate emotional responses. Select a time when both parents can be present for a reasonable amount of time after the conversation, ensuring the children feel safe and heard. Avoid telling them during a period of other upheavals, such as right before moving house, starting a new school term, or around important holidays. I would also strongly recommend informing your children's school, childcare provider, and the parents of their close friends soon after you share the news with them. This ensures that they are being cared for through this transition, even when they are in the care of others. But more on this in the next chapter.

MISTAKE #10: COMBINING THE ANNOUNCEMENT WITH A HAPPY MOMENT

It isn't uncommon for people to consider telling their children about the divorce during a time where they feel they will be in a good mood and the news will be softened by the joy of the day. While that might seem like a good idea, it is actually advisable to avoid sharing news of a divorce during happy moments, like Christmas or a birthday, because these are times meant to create positive, lasting memories. Breaking such difficult news during a festive or special occasion can create a painful association with that day, overshadowing the joy and togetherness of such moments. Instead, it's important to choose a quieter, more neutral time when children can fully absorb the news with the support they need, without having to mask or navigate their feelings during a celebration.

② FRAMING THE CONVERSATION

It is important to present the divorce as a mutual decision, even if it isn't. Avoid blaming each other or involving your children in the reasons for the separation, as this can create confusion, loyalty conflicts, and guilt.

Tailor the conversation to the age and emotional maturity of your children (see further on in this chapter for age-specific guidance). Younger children need simple, concrete explanations, while older children may want more information and have more specific questions. Be prepared for different reactions, as each child will digest the news in their own way and time. Some may express sadness, anger, or fear, while others might initially seem indifferent.

Most parents, in the context of their divorce, make the mistake of either over-involving their children or not talking to them about it at all. Neither option is ideal of course, and it is sometimes a fine line to walk.

I have never met a parent who claimed not to want to protect their children during their divorce, yet it is far too common to see parents involving the children in their divorce feuds. For example, I had a client whose spouse read their court orders to their young children and replayed everything that had been said at court hearings. Parents experiencing divorce must learn to find their own age-appropriate sources of support to avoid relying on their children. One recent example I would share here came from one of my clients who was really struggling to accept her husband's infidelity. She felt strongly that her children should know the reason for their divorce and understand that it was "his fault". The need for vindication is completely natural, as is the need to feel like there was some sense of moral justice in this situation. Unfortunately, it really isn't for the children to be providing judgement or taking sides. Children are half of each of their parents, and hearing about the wrongdoings of either one of them can be extremely harmful to their sense of self-worth. So, while you want to be honest and open with your children, also be aware of what topics are unhelpful to them and need to remain solely between their parents.

EXPERT TIP

In preparing to speak to your children about the divorce, there are five golden rules to keep in mind:

- Be honest (but only tell them what they need to know)
- Don't assign blame for the divorce
- Make the message age-appropriate
- Keep the conversation open
- Provide ongoing reassurance

③ ACKNOWLEDGE THEIR FEELINGS AND ADDRESS THEIR QUESTIONS

Whatever their age, children often need reassurance when faced with the news of divorce. Reassure them that nothing they did caused the decision. Repeat this message as often as necessary to help them internalise it.

Let your children know it's normal to have a range of emotions and encourage them to express how they feel. Whether they are angry, confused, or upset, validate their feelings by letting them know it's okay to feel that way. Encourage open communication and let them know they can come to you with any questions or concerns at any time.

Expect that your children will have many questions and answer them as honestly as possible while keeping their emotional maturity in mind. They will want to know how the divorce will affect their daily lives—where they will live, whether they will still see both parents, and how routines such as school, activities, and friendships will be impacted. Being able to provide clear and consistent answers can help alleviate some of their anxiety. In the upcoming pages, I will share some specific questions children are likely to ask depending on their age group. Once again, the more you can prepare in advance, the better equipped you will be to answer your children's questions in a calm and reassuring manner. Make sure your answers align with those of your spouse beforehand. I spend a lot of time with my clients role-playing various reactions and coaching them on how to respond in a comforting yet honest way. Remember that it is developmentally appropriate for your children to view your divorce from a very self-focused perspective. Their questions are therefore likely to centre around how it will impact them personally rather than how you are feeling.

It is important to be honest about what you know and don't know at this stage. In most cases, the details of the child arrangements and where each parent will live will not have been ironed out completely. It is absolutely acceptable to tell your children that you haven't yet decided on every detail but reassure them that you will let them know as things evolve and consider their point of view. When you can, do provide certainty on those aspects that you and your spouse have already agreed to.

(4) REASSURE THEM OF STABILITY AND LOVE

Children whose parents are divorcing often fear that their lives will become unpredictable or unstable. It's important to reassure them that while some things will change, much will remain the same. Be specific in your message, providing details and certainty where you can, as this will help ease any anxiety your children may be experiencing and lessen any sense of instability. If the children are still living at home, try to keep their routines as consistent as possible, including school, extracurricular activities, and time with friends. Children of all ages find comfort in familiar patterns, so maintaining stability will help them feel more secure.

It's also vital to stress the fact that they will continue to have a relationship with both parents, even though you won't be living together anymore. Emphasise that your love for them is unwavering and that both of you will always be there to support them.

EXPERT TIP

I often suggest that my clients create a calendar for their children, to reassure them that both of their parents will have ongoing involvement in their lives. For younger children, this can include photos of each parent on days when they will see them. For older ones, it can be a shared family calendar in an app such as Google Calendar or Our Family Wizard. The point is to create a visual representation of when they will see each parent to help them understand that both parents remain part of their daily life.

⑤ FOLLOW-UP CONVERSATIONS

The initial conversation is just the beginning. Your children will likely need ongoing support and additional talks as they continue to take in all the implications of your divorce. They may have questions weeks or even months later, or they may only express certain feelings once the changes begin to take effect. Be patient and available, offering reassurance and stability at every step.

I would strongly recommend that your spouse and yourself work together to monitor the children's behaviour in the weeks and months that follow in order to quickly address any concerns. It might be a good idea to have a weekly check-in to discuss potential changes in the children's behaviour, any concerns they have expressed and how you can address these. If you find that your children are struggling with the divorce, consider seeking external support, such as a child therapist who can help them navigate their emotions in a constructive way.

⑥ WHAT TO SAY DEPENDING ON THEIR AGE

As I have said above, the way you will present things and the questions the children are likely to ask will vary significantly based on their maturity. If you have children of very different ages, or with very different personalities/needs, it may be worth considering speaking to them individually so you can tailor the conversation to their needs. Make sure there is no major time lapse between speaking to each of them as you don't want them to hear the news from each other. One of my clients recently contacted me for help informing her youngest daughter of her divorce. For logistical reasons, her ex-husband was set on telling each of their children at different stages of the divorce journey, leading to the youngest not being informed until after they were actually divorced! You can easily imagine how this 18-year-old felt when she not only learned that her parents had been divorcing for the past year without her knowing, but also that all her siblings were already aware of the situation.

Should you have children with special needs or learning difficulties, I would strongly recommend engaging with a specialist prior to sharing the news with them, as the advice below might not apply.

Toddlers

MISTAKE #11: NOT INFORMING TODDLERS BECAUSE THEY ARE TOO YOUNG TO UNDERSTAND

I have had several clients over the years ask me whether they even needed to tell their children as they were "too young to understand". The answer is a resounding YES! Even if your children are not verbal yet or seem unable to take in the news, they need to be told about the change. This avoids anxiety and helps them prepare for some things to be different. I remember reading a book during my pregnancy where the therapist advised to inform babies of changes as well, for example if you were going on a trip or having visitors. No matter the age, the children will absorb the tension and change of energy in the home.

I speak from experience when I talk about announcing divorce decisions to toddlers - my own children were 2 and 4 years old when we separated. At the time, we spoke to a child therapist for advice, which proved very helpful. There were two main pieces of advice she gave us that stuck with me:

1- Tell the truth: Don't sugar-coat it or pretend it is temporary when you know it is not. Simply explain that you (their parents) are no longer in love and would like to live separately from now on. Keep the message simple and straightforward. No need to say much more. If it feels like they are receptive to more information, you can explain in simple terms what this means in practice for them. Something along the lines of

"Mummy and Daddy have decided to live in different homes because we can't be happy living together anymore, but we both love you very much and that will never change.". Reassure them that they will continue to see both parents regularly (if that is the case) but do not dwell on logistics and details as they are probably too young to retain any of that information.

2- Talk to them about love: As I mentioned earlier in this chapter, it is essential to reassure your children of all ages of your love for them at all stages of the divorce. With very young children, it will likely be the first time they become aware that love can end. This can lead to them suddenly worrying that since you stopped loving Mummy or Daddy, you might also one day stop loving them. Explaining to them that parents are people from different families who have chosen to love each other and how different that is from the love a parent feels for their child will help clarify. The point here is to help them understand that not all love ends, and that the love bond that exists between parents and children does not end in the same way romantic love might. Again, keep it simple and use age-appropriate vocabulary, but make it clear to them that your love for them will never end.

The younger the children, the shorter the conversation is likely to be. Choose a time when you can have their full attention (not when they are tired, playing or otherwise distracted). In many cases, the first question toddlers ask after this announcement is "Can I go play now?". The answer is "Yes". It doesn't matter if you haven't said everything you wanted to say. This is their way of saying "I can't deal with this right now". Give them time and space but continue to offer to answer their questions or concerns in the weeks and months that follow.

TYPICAL QUESTIONS FROM A TODDLER

- Will I still see you both?
- Where will I live?
- Did I do something wrong?
- Are you still my Mummy/Daddy?

Children aged 4-12

This is a very wide age group but covers most of what we typically think of as childhood. A four-year-old will of course not process emotions or express their feelings in the same way a 12-year-old would, so the guidance below needs to be adjusted depending on your children's age and maturity.

In most cases, children in this age group have enough cognitive development to understand that a significant change is happening, but their emotional responses and comprehension levels vary widely. While they can understand explanations about how their lives might change (e.g., where they'll live or who will pick them up from school), they may not fully grasp the long-term implications of divorce.

When speaking to children aged 4-12, it's helpful to provide simple but honest explanations, focusing on what will stay the same and offering reassurances about family stability. They may ask "why" questions that require a bit more depth, so a gentle, clear response like, "Sometimes adults are happier living apart," can work well. Children in this age group may also show concern about how the divorce affects their day-to-day life, so practical details about routines help them feel more in control and secure. Clarify logistics that you have already defined: where they will live, how they will see each parent, and which routines will stay the same. You could say, "You'll have two homes now. You'll still go to the same school, and your routines will stay similar. You'll see both of us regularly." Reassure them that they'll still enjoy time with both parents in ways they're used to, focusing on what will remain familiar.

> "Some parents, when they're angry, get along much better when they don't live together."
>
> *Robin Williams in Mrs. Doubtfire*

It's also natural for children to wonder if the divorce could be temporary. They might ask, "Will you ever get back together?" A kind but clear response could be, "No, we won't be getting back together. But we'll both still be here for you in different homes." This answer sets a realistic expectation while gently acknowledging their hope.

Some children, especially around 8-12, may mistakenly believe they had a role in the separation. Address this by saying, "Nothing you did caused this. Divorce is an adult decision between us [your parents], and it's never because of anything a child does or doesn't do." Sometimes children relate your decision to divorce to a specific incident they remember, such as an argument in the car or something they did to their sibling. You need to make it very clear that their behaviour is not responsible for the breakup and that your decision is not based on a single argument or event.

TYPICAL QUESTIONS FROM A YOUNG CHILD

- Why are you getting a divorce?
- Whose fault is it?
- Where will I live?
- What will happen on my birthday?
- Will you get back together?

Teenagers

With adolescents, parental concerns are often exacerbated by the developmental and physical changes their teens are already experiencing more or less smoothly. Parents tend to be acutely aware of the formative significance of teenage years and often have a deeper fear of causing long-term damage as adolescents move toward adulthood.

Empirical studies[23] highlight the ongoing significance of parental support and the value of strong sibling relationships for adolescents during this period. There are two golden rules when it comes to supporting your teenager through your divorce:

1. Let them be kids: One of the common mistakes divorcing parents make is to treat their teenagers as adults. Parentification can take many forms, from asking your teen to take on new household responsibilities to caring for siblings or providing emotional support to their grieving parent.

Teenagers are typically very reliant on interactions with their friends and can be heavily preoccupied with social dynamics at school. Understandably, they might not feel like the divorce is taking over their life in the same way it is for their parents. It is healthy for them to continue to

---

[23] See "Adolescent Adjustment to Parental Marital Transitions: Experiences in Urban, Rural and Suburban Communities" by Carrie Krug, Family Transition, November 2024.

spend time with friends and to pursue age-appropriate activities. The divorce might be overhauling their parents' world, but it doesn't need to do so for adolescent children as well.

2. Let them choose who to get support from: Contrary to young children who will generally gravitate toward one or both of their parents for support, adolescents usually have access to more options outside of the household.

Young adults might be much more interested in spending time with their peers than their parents, or they may be naturally drawn toward other adult figures, be it aunts and uncles, teachers, coaches, or mental health professionals. The importance of sibling solidarity in these times of stress must also be acknowledged, as brothers and sisters often become closer through the shared experience of their parents' divorce.

A word of caution, though: keep an eye out for less healthy sources of support such as dubious online communities or those that appear to be encouraging unhealthy or risky behaviours. Keep the flow of communication going and get professional support if you feel that you or your child needs it.

TYPICAL QUESTIONS FROM TEENAGERS

- Where will I live and will I need to change schools?
- Which parent is responsible for the breakup?
- How will this affect family traditions, like holidays and celebrations?
- Will I still see you both?
- Are you both going to be ok?

Grown up children

With the rise of "Gray divorce",[24] ie divorce among people aged 50+, more and more of my clients are approaching me about informing their grown-up children about the divorce. The good news is that statistics show that divorces later in life are less acrimonious and more amicable, meaning the message to the children is usually more positive. [25]

However, with children who are now living independently, their parents' decision to divorce may come as a huge surprise because they have not been privy to the tensions and unhappiness that likely led to their

[24] A Pew Research Center study published on March 9, 2017 shows that the divorce rate for Americans aged 50 and older roughly doubled between 1990 and 2015. For adults aged 65 and older, the rate tripled during the same period.

[25] A study from Bowling Green State University's National Center for Family & Marriage Research indicates that gray divorces are generally less contentious because older couples often cite "growing apart" rather than intense disputes or infidelity as reasons for separation.

decision. It may therefore take them a while to come to terms with the announcement. Assuming that grown-up children who have moved out of the family home won't be affected by their parents' divorce is a common mistake, as it overlooks the deep impact that a family breakup can have on adults as well. Yes, they will not have to split their time between two homes, but their identity and sense of stability is likely to be shaken. Divorce can often lead them to feelings of grief, confusion, and loss of a family unit they thought was permanent. Unfortunately, age doesn't make one immune to the emotional effects of parental separation.

There are two other elements to consider when speaking to your adult children about your decision to divorce:

1- They are themselves starting or about to start their own serious romantic relationships: As your children grow up and begin their own lives, they are often also beginning to explore more long-term relationships. Whether good or bad, their parents' marriage will be their main point of reference with regards to what a love relationship looks like. The announcement of the end of your marriage may therefore shake many of the foundations on which they will have begun to create their own romantic relationships. This might directly challenge their own beliefs about love, commitment, and trust. You will need to be aware of this and to give them time to digest the news. Make yourself available to discuss their concerns whenever they need you.

2- They might feel a new sense of responsibility: In many cases, children who have already flown the nest are mostly focused on building their own life and career. Hearing about your divorce may suddenly lead to a new sense of responsibility to support each parent emotionally and, in some cases, practically. Beware of placing your children in a role reversal situation, where they feel obligated to act as a mediator, confidant, or even a caretaker, especially if one parent seems more vulnerable or alone. They may be adults, but they will always be children in their relationship with you.

TYPICAL QUESTIONS FROM GROWN-UP CHILDREN

- When did you make this decision?
- What led to this decision?
- What does this mean in terms of family finances or assets?
- How will this affect family traditions and dynamics?
- Is there anything you need from me during this transition?

Chapter 7: How do I tell others?

In a nutshell

1. Set clear boundaries: who, when, what.
2. Shield yourself from the judgement and opinions of others.
3. Divorce will impact your professional life, so consider informing your employer.

There are a number of people you will need to inform of the divorce. As things evolve, you will eventually want to share the news with your family and friends, maybe even your employer. All these people will need time to grasp the news and understand what it means for them. By planning the conversation ahead of time, just as you did with your spouse and children, you can help minimise misunderstandings and avoid adding unnecessary emotional strain on both yourself and them.

If you are an expat, sharing the news with your friends and family in your home country must be handled with care given the distance that separates you. You might also consider telling people you know locally, with whom you think you can share your feelings even if they are not yet very close friends. Sometimes, showing vulnerability is a good way to solidify friendships and feel closer to others.

Sharing the news with friends and family

Telling friends and family about your divorce can feel like a daunting task, especially when you consider the reactions you might receive. In general, it is advisable to share the news with them in person if you can as it will help you manage their reaction in real time. An intimate conversation can also be a way of fostering mutual support and of being clear on what they can do to help you during this time. Here are a few suggestions on how to approach this.

1 SELECTING WHO TO INFORM

The first step is to decide who truly needs to know. It's natural to inform those closest to you, such as immediate family members or your closest friends, but beyond that, the choice is entirely yours. Start by thinking about the people who will provide you with the support and understanding you need during this time. Close family members and friends are often the most appropriate people to tell first, as they are likely to be emotionally invested in your wellbeing. They may also be the ones who will notice changes in your life, so it makes sense to keep them informed.

However, you don't need to rush to tell everyone in your social or professional circles. If you feel you need more time before sharing the news, it's perfectly fine to keep things private for a while.

There may also be practical considerations when deciding who to tell about your divorce. For example, as I mentioned in Chapter 6, if you have children with your ex-partner, you may need to talk with teachers or childcare providers, particularly if your child's routines or emotional state are affected. Being selective about who knows ensures that only those who can actively support your circumstances are informed.

Similarly, if you are living abroad, you may choose to share the news with your family and friends in your home country face to face next time you see them, rather than on the phone.

You may find it helpful to keep a list of the people you have informed so you don't lose track and to avoid having to retell your painful story more than necessary.

(2) FRAMING THE CONVERSATION

When it comes to framing the conversation, try to keep it simple and straightforward. Be honest without delving into too much detail. It's entirely up to you how much you want to disclose. Some people may prefer to provide the full story, while others might only want to share the basic facts. You could start with something like, "I wanted to let you know that [spouse's name] and I have decided to divorce. It wasn't an easy decision, but we believe it's the best choice for both of us."

By framing the conversation in a neutral tone, you're setting the stage for how others should respond. You might also find it useful to request some understanding, saying, "I would appreciate your support while I navigate this new chapter." When you begin informing people, keep in mind that other friends or family members may expect to be told once they find out the news has been shared with others. You might be asked, "Have you told [another person] yet?" or even face a certain level of surprise if someone close to you learns the news from a third party. However, it's important to manage these expectations and remain firm in your right to control the flow of information. You can set boundaries with people by saying something like, "I'm taking my time sharing this with others, and I'd appreciate it if you kept this private for now." This gives you space to approach the situation on your own terms, without feeling rushed or pressured into informing everyone at once.

Moreover, you are not required to offer regular updates about the progression of your divorce. Divorce can be a lengthy and complex journey, and some people may enquire frequently about how things are going. Again, it's up to you to decide how much information you want to provide. If you find frequent enquiries overwhelming, you can politely let others know that you'll share updates when you're ready, saying something like, "It's a work in progress, and I'll let you know when there's something new." As we discussed in Chapter 4, friends and family can be intrinsically biased and therefore provide unhelpful advice during your divorce. Remember to keep your loved ones close for emotional support but keep in mind the limitations that come with their advice: they are not professionals, their experiences might not be relevant to yours and they will have an emotional bias in your situation which might inflame conflict further.

③ HANDLING DIFFICULT QUESTIONS AND JUDGEMENT

Difficult questions are almost inevitable when discussing divorce. You might hear things like, "What happened?" or "Whose decision was it?" These questions can feel invasive, especially if you're still coming to terms with the situation yourself. The key here is to establish boundaries early on. Remember that you are not obliged to answer every question. If someone asks something you're uncomfortable responding to, it's perfectly acceptable to say, "That's personal, and I'd rather not go into detail right now." Redirect the conversation if necessary, focusing on the future rather than the past: "Right now, I'm focusing on moving forward and adjusting to the changes."

If the conversation turns to assumptions or blame, gently correct the course by reminding others that divorce is rarely black and white. A phrase like "This wasn't about one person being wrong or right – we simply grew apart and believe this is the best way forward" can help neutralise judgement.

Family and friends might express disappointment, or worse, judgement. It's important to remember that other people's views do not define your experience. When confronted with judgement, remain firm and confident in your decision. You have no obligation to justify your decision nor is it your responsibility to convince others that you are making the right decision. You could say, "I understand this might be difficult for you to accept, but I've made the choice that's right for me." This acknowledges their concerns without allowing them to undermine your confidence.

Although it can be difficult when you are already feeling emotionally shaken, try not to take judgement personally; often it comes from fear, ignorance, or their own biases. Some people may never fully understand your decision, and that's okay. Focus on those who offer support and respect your choices.

Keep in mind that cultural and religious views can also play a significant role in how divorce is perceived. In some cultures, divorce is seen as a failure or a source of shame, and this can lead to added pressure from family members to stay in the marriage. Likewise, religious communities may have strong views on marriage and separation, and navigating these can be especially difficult if your faith or cultural background is important to you. When sharing the news with those whose views may differ from yours, it can help to acknowledge the cultural or religious lens through which they see divorce, while also standing by your decision. For example, "I know our culture values marriage highly, and I've considered this carefully, but I believe this is the best decision for my wellbeing." It's crucial to remember that while cultural or religious beliefs are deeply important, your emotional health and future should not be sacrificed to meet external expectations.

Another common concern I hear from my clients is the fear of gossip or others spreading the news before you're ready. While this can be frustrating, try to control what you can. Speak to those you trust and kindly ask them to respect your privacy by not sharing your situation with others. Most people will understand the sensitivity of the matter and respect your wishes, but if the news does spread, don't feel pressured to address it publicly. In some cases, it can be helpful to acknowledge the situation without feeling obliged to give additional details. If you hear that others have learned about your divorce through unofficial channels, you can address it calmly with, "Yes, it's true that we're getting a divorce. I'm handling it privately right now but thank you for your concern."

(4) PROTECTING YOUR EMOTIONAL WELL-BEING

Finally, be kind to yourself throughout this transition. Divorce is emotionally draining, and sharing the news can be just as challenging as the divorce itself. Surround yourself with people who lift you up, and don't hesitate to seek professional help such as a therapist or divorce coach to guide you through these conversations. Remember, this is your journey, and only yours.

(5) HANDLING THE IMPACT OF DIVORCE ON FRIENDSHIPS

There is no reason why friends would need to choose who to align with, as they are not part of the marital relationship. But in practice, this is usually a very sore point for divorcing couples, who often feel that a lack of allegiance is a form of betrayal. This emanates from the overwhelming sense of vulnerability and loneliness that comes during these types of life transitions. When we feel unsupported and everything is changing around us, we need the people we love to hold steady and be there for us.

Each individual in a couple has two categories of friends: those who are mostly or exclusively theirs, and those who they share with their spouse. The ones that are truly yours will naturally stay by your side and usually stop seeing your soon-to-be-ex. The problems arise when it comes to friends you have in common. In this respect, there are two main things to keep in mind:

Be clear about your needs

Most good friends will want to be there for you and give you the support you require during your separation. They will, however, probably struggle to figure out what exactly you want from them.

In most cases, what we need from our friends at this time is someone we can speak to without fear of being judged, someone who helps us take our mind off things. Your friends will be able to offer you this, whether they are still friends with your ex or not. Where you can help them, though, is by being clear on what you expect from them.

It may be that you prefer for them to simply listen, or that you want to be distracted from the divorce and not talk about it at all.

Similarly, if they are still in contact with your ex, you may want to ask them not to mention his or her name or to share information about you with them. By providing clarity to your friends about the ways in which they can be there for you, you are making it easier for them to do so and avoiding frustrations later down the line.

It would make sense to ask them in return if there is anything they would like you to avoid doing because it makes them feel uncomfortable. Speaking badly about your ex might just be one of the things they ask you to avoid doing in their presence.

Trust the benefits of time: your real friends will emerge

The final lesson is probably the most important one. True friends reveal themselves in times of crisis. Whether they stay in contact with your ex or not, those who are worthy of your trust and affection are those who will remain by your side during this difficult period.

By remaining confident that time will naturally weed out those who were not truly your friends, you will take a lot of pressure off yourself, and them. You may end up being hurt and disappointed by those who you thought were close friends and are failing you at this time. But there will also likely be some pleasant surprises with regards to other friends who will actually step up to the plate.

Through the uncoupling process, you are also likely to meet new people or to reconnect with old hobbies which will expand your social circle. Over time, you will start building a whole series of new friendships with people your ex has never even met.

The good news is that time will do the work for you; these things will happen naturally. Focusing on the friends you have gained and the relationships you have reinforced during your divorce will improve your ability to start the next chapter of your life with confidence. Trust that in the end, it won't matter who stayed in touch with your ex or not.

MISTAKE #12: ASKING YOUR FRIENDS TO TAKE SIDES

One of the most common feelings your friends will be experiencing during this time is discomfort. Even if you do not ask them to, they will feel like they are being expected to take sides.

It may seem obvious, but it is essential to reassure them that that is not the case. While the divorce will usually involve some conflict in the couple that is separating, it is healthier for everyone if they can keep that conflict between themselves.

Just like it is always recommended not to ask children to choose between one or another of their parents, friends should not be made to choose either. Similarly, you cannot blame your friends for not hating your ex when he or she hasn't done anything to them personally. Expecting loyalty at all costs is an unreasonable demand which often causes much resentment and unnecessary ending of friendships.

By reassuring your friends that you respect their neutrality, you will see two amazing things happen. First, they are much more likely to remain closer to the person who is not making them take sides and is therefore sparing them the discomfort of hearing about all the horrible things your ex has done. Keep in mind that no one ever looks good trying to make someone else look bad. Second, you will notice that by not speaking ill of your ex to your friends, you will start letting go of your anger and stop thinking about it as much. Divorce is a period in which we often need support and distractions.

Our friends and family are in a unique position to offer us some of that relief and are therefore extremely valuable during divorce. However, when it comes to processing your feelings, planning your divorce strategy, or understanding the lessons learned, it is better to seek professional support.

Informing your employer

While discussing such a personal matter with your employer might feel uncomfortable, it is often necessary for several reasons. Below I will share my advice, based on my experience as a divorce coach, as to why and how you should inform your employer.

① WHY INFORM YOUR EMPLOYER ABOUT YOUR DIVORCE?

Impact on work performance

In these post-Covid days with many of us now working remotely, our personal and professional lives are intertwined more than ever before. It is therefore not surprising that stressful experiences such as divorce or separation have an increased impact on our performance at work.

Some of us may not realise, however, the scale of disruption this causes. A recent study by Rayden Solicitors found that 79% of employees feel that their divorce had an impact on their ability to work.[26] A similar study by the Nashville Business Journal estimated that employee productivity falls by 40% during the first six months of divorce. For one year after the divorce, employee productivity remains down 20%; co-workers lose 2%; and the supervisor loses 1%. According to the study, productivity continues to suffer on some level for seven years![27]

---

[26] See the 2021 Divorce in the Workplace UK study by Rayden Solicitors
[27] The cost of divorce to employers, by Rosemary Frank, March 10, 2014

By informing your employer about your situation, you provide context for any changes in your behaviour or performance. This allows your employer to potentially offer support or adjustments during this difficult period. Of course, if you don't feel like the quality of your relationship with them will lead to this type of support, you may decide that it is best not to inform them of the latest events in your personal life.

Legal and financial implications

Divorce often comes with legal and financial complexities that may require time off work. Court hearings, meetings with lawyers, and the division of assets can be time-consuming and may require you to take leave at short notice. If your employer is aware of your situation, they are more likely to be understanding and accommodating of your need for flexibility.

Moreover, certain aspects of your employment, such as pension schemes, life insurance policies and tax codes may need to be updated following a divorce. Your employer's HR department can assist with these changes, but only if they are aware of your circumstances.

Mental health considerations

The emotional strain of a divorce can take a toll on your mental health, potentially leading to conditions such as anxiety or depression. Many workplaces now recognise the importance of mental health and offer support through Employee Assistance Programmes (EAPs) or mental health days. By informing your employer about your divorce, you open the door to accessing these resources which could prove invaluable.

Maintaining professional relationships

Keeping your employer in the loop can help maintain trust and transparency in your professional relationship. If your work is affected by your personal life, and you haven't communicated this, it could lead to misunderstandings or a negative perception of your commitment to your role. Being upfront about your situation helps to manage expectations and maintain a positive working relationship.

② HOW TO INFORM YOUR EMPLOYER

Once you've decided to inform your employer, it's essential to approach the conversation thoughtfully. Here are some steps to guide you:

1. Choose the right time and setting

Just as with your spouse or children, the timing of the conversation is crucial. When discussing personal matters at work, it's advisable to choose a time when both you and your employer are not under significant stress or pressure, such as during a major project deadline. Arrange a private meeting rather than bringing it up in a casual or public setting. This ensures that the conversation remains confidential and allows both parties to focus on the discussion.

2. Prepare what to say

Before the meeting, take some time to think about what you want to say. Be clear and concise, focusing on how the divorce might impact your work rather than delving into personal details. For example, you could say, "I wanted to inform you that I am currently going through a divorce. This might affect my availability for work or my concentration at times. I wanted to make you aware so that we can discuss how best to handle this."

3. Discuss any necessary adjustments

Depending on your situation, you may need to discuss temporary adjustments to your work schedule or responsibilities. This could include flexible working hours, remote work, or a temporary reduction in workload. Be open to suggestions from your employer and try to reach a solution that works for both parties.

Taking time off work or reducing your workload can be an enormous relief when you are dealing with a whirlwind of emotions and divorce-related activities, but committing to your usual workload can also be a good way of staying grounded in a steady routine and offer you a sense of purpose. A prolonged absence from work might also make it more difficult to reengage in normal routines after the divorce. It is ultimately for you to decide what the best way forward is for you, depending on your emotional and physical capacities of the moment.

4. Consider involving human resources

In some cases, it may be beneficial to involve your HR department in the discussion. HR professionals are trained to handle sensitive situations and can provide additional support, such as explaining your rights and entitlements, or assisting with paperwork related to changes in your personal circumstances.

5. Follow up

After the initial conversation, it's important to follow up with your employer or HR to keep them informed of any changes in your situation. This could involve updating them on court dates, changes to your availability, or any other factors that might impact your work. Regular communication helps to maintain transparency and ensures that your employer can continue to support you effectively.

Chapter 8: What happens next?

Recently, one of my clients described to me how she felt now that she had finalised all her preparation before speaking to her spouse: she said it felt like those few seconds of suspense when you are on a rollercoaster and have just completed the long ascent to the top. Just before the big drop, there are a few seconds where you are held suspended over emptiness, anticipating the drop to come. Once the rollercoaster car actually proceeds, you are on the ride and it all goes well. But those few seconds before reality hits are specially designed to make you anticipate the fear.

Taking the first step towards making your divorce decision a reality is very similar. You will have spent weeks, months, maybe even years, preparing for this event and it will now be just ahead of you. This can easily trigger a case of "cold feet" and often leads my clients to suddenly reconsider their decision. It is absolutely normal to feel fear. Up until that point, divorce was a very theoretical conversation. If after careful consideration you have still opted to divorce, the decision is now finally going to hit home.

So now that you have followed all the steps outlined in this book, what do you do next? Your main objective during the next phase is managing the business of divorce in the best way possible for you.

There is no way of sugar-coating the fact that this is often the hardest part of your divorce. Tensions will be riding high, big decisions will need to be made and the family's structure will be redefined. It is therefore essential that you ensure your own resilience and strength during this unsettled time. This will come through three main wellbeing priorities:

- Your ability to manage change and uncertainty.
- Your strength in setting boundaries and preserving your mental health.
- Your focus on your own self-care during this upheaval.

Managing change and uncertainty

1 PREPARING YOURSELF FOR CHANGE

Divorce and separation bring with them a tsunami of changes: a new relationship status, a new family setup, possibly a new house, a new household income, and sometimes even a new job, new country or new friends. This often feels overwhelming to people experiencing such profound shifts, and they may feel that dealing with such turmoil is too difficult.

As human beings, we often struggle to accept change, even when we know deep down that it's necessary. This is especially true during divorce, when the life we've built and become accustomed to suddenly shifts in ways we never imagined. The routine of shared responsibilities, even the small comforts of a daily life together, can feel like anchors that keep us from stepping into the unknown. Adjusting to new roles—co-parent instead of spouse, single person instead of partner—can feel disorienting and overwhelming. We cling to what we know, even when the change could lead to a healthier, more fulfilling future. The emotional weight of letting go often makes us resist the very transformations that are needed to heal and grow.

However, so often, I realise that my clients completely underestimate their ability to deal with change. Our status quo bias leads us to assume that a bad situation is better than an unknown one. However, once you take some time to identify the inner resources you possess that help you deal with change (sometimes unconsciously!), a true sense of empowerment emerges. If you feel that handling numerous changes will be difficult for you, I encourage you to look at past experiences of change and mark which of the examples in the boxes below you have experienced.

Having children	**Death in the family**	**Marriage**
Health problems	**World events**	**Move abroad**
Redundancy	**Promotion**	**New team**

Thinking back to these events, I encourage you to reflect on how you navigated them at the time:

1. How did you feel while you were experiencing this change?
2. How did the change affect you in the short term?

3. How did it affect you in the long term?
4. What did you do to help you navigate the change?
5. Are these resources, or similar ones, available to you today in the context of your divorce or separation?
6. What can you do to mobilise these resources now?

(2) ACCEPTING UNCERTAINTY

I often hear clients complain about their inability to make plans such as holidays or professional changes because they don't know what their life will look like post-divorce. Sometimes it is those smaller things that really get to us and make us feel stuck in a limbo throughout the divorce process.

To cope with this uncertainty, it's crucial to focus on what you can control (see the Circles of control diagram on the next page). Reading this book is an excellent first step in that direction. Break up the many pieces of advice I shared into bitesize pieces and start setting small, manageable goals for yourself, such as creating a budget or exploring housing options. You will likely notice that this gives you a sense of progress and control. As we discussed in Chapter 4, seeking the right emotional support is also key; talking to a therapist or joining a support group can help you navigate the turmoil and gain perspective. Sometimes, just being able to vent your frustration or share your feelings with someone who understands you is a great source of relief.

CIRCLES OF CONTROL

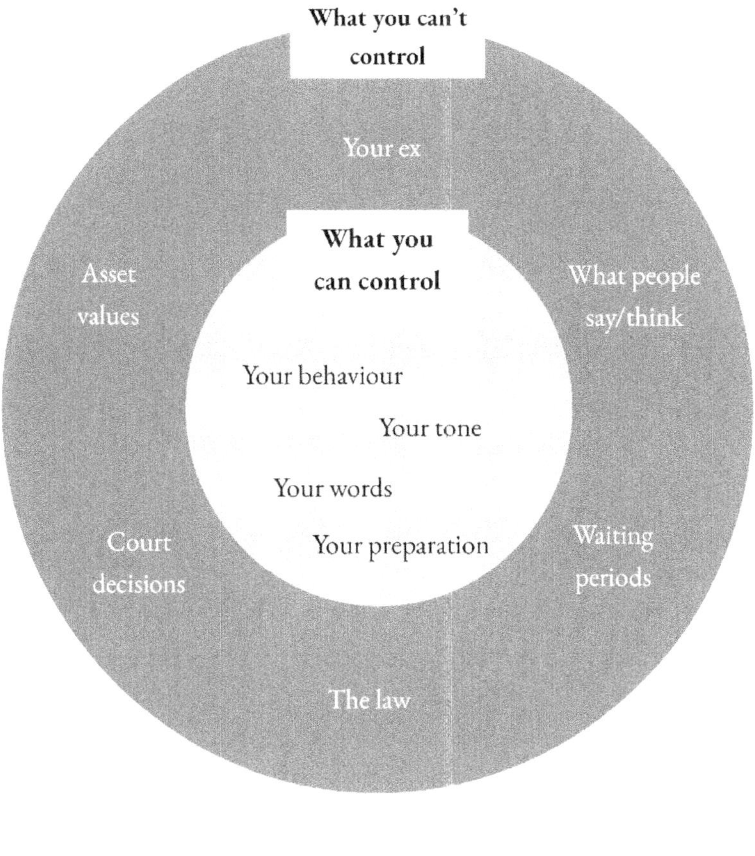

Setting boundaries

One of the best ways to help you preserve your sense of stability during divorce is to set clear, healthy boundaries. Whether with your friends and family or your soon-to-be-ex spouse, boundaries are essential to protect your mental space, avoid unnecessary conflict, and ensure you can get through the divorce in a way that works best for you.

1 BOUNDARIES WITH YOUR SOON-TO-BE-EX

Setting boundaries with your spouse is crucial to protect your emotional health and create a smoother path for the divorce. Without clear boundaries, you risk falling into patterns of argument, emotional manipulation, or unnecessary stress. Here are a few key boundaries to set with your ex.

Communication boundaries

It's important to establish clear communication guidelines, particularly if there are children involved. Agree on a preferred method of communication—whether it's email, text, or a parenting app—and set rules around the times or topics that can be discussed. This helps prevent emotions from spilling into every conversation.

For example, you could agree to only communicate about child arrangements through email, and limit phone calls to emergencies. When setting this boundary, be assertive but respectful: "For now, I think it's best we only discuss parenting matters through email so that everything is clear and recorded."

Emotional boundaries

Divorce can bring out emotions from the past, including unresolved conflicts or ongoing tension. Set firm boundaries that limit emotional entanglements. This might involve refusing to engage in arguments or walking away from conversations that become heated. Keep interactions focused on practical matters rather than getting drawn into discussions about the past or blaming each other.

A good way to assert this boundary is by saying, "I don't want to argue about this. Let's focus on finding a solution for the children."

Physical boundaries

If you and your spouse will share a home during the divorce or will frequently meet due to co-parenting, setting physical boundaries is vital. For example, you could choose to limit face-to-face interactions to only what is strictly necessary, perhaps leveraging Shuttle Mediation, where you and your spouse do not sit together in the same room during sessions, but instead, the mediator goes back and forth between you as a middle person. You can also arrange for your divorce coach or a friend to join you as a moderator. If discussing the divorce in person is too emotionally difficult, rely more on written communication.

2 BOUNDARIES WITH FRIENDS AND FAMILY

Setting boundaries with your loved ones is necessary for your own peace of mind. Here are three things to keep in mind:

Define what you're comfortable sharing

Decide early on what parts of your private life you're comfortable discussing and what you'd prefer to keep to yourself. It's perfectly reasonable to keep the specifics of your legal proceedings, financial arrangements, or emotional state private. Once you've made this decision, you can politely tell people when certain topics are off-limits.

You could say, for example: "I really appreciate your concern, but I'd rather not discuss the details of the divorce at the moment. I'll let you know if I need support."

Set time limits on conversations

In the throes of divorce, everyone might want to offer their perspective or hear the latest updates. However, having the same conversations over and over can become emotionally exhausting. Set limits by politely ending conversations when you feel they're becoming repetitive or unproductive.

You might say something like, "Thank you for asking, but I'd prefer to focus on other things right now".

Limit unsolicited advice

Friends and family, even with the best intentions, may bombard you with advice that isn't always helpful or applicable. This can lead to added pressure, especially if they're pushing you in a direction that doesn't feel right.

A gentle way to set this boundary is to acknowledge their concern while asserting your own decisions: "I know you want the best for me, and I'm considering my options carefully. Right now, I need to trust the route I've chosen" or "I've got a very good divorce team and am taking their advice. Thanks for your opinion though".

(3) BOUNDARIES WITH YOURSELF

Lastly, setting boundaries with yourself is just as important as setting them with others. It is easy to get caught up in feelings of guilt, regret, or disappointment during a divorce. Give yourself permission to take breaks, to step back when things feel too overwhelming, and to focus on your own healing. Resist the urge to check in on your spouse through social media or mutual friends—these actions can keep you emotionally tied to the past and make it harder to move forward.

Self-care

As I mentioned before, research shows that divorce is the second most stressful life experience a person can go through, just after the death of a spouse.[28] Divorce involves a complex and unfamiliar legal process, extensive decision-making and enormous uncertainty. It is also an emotional trauma, an experience that often comes with a sense of loss, bereavement for the life you had envisaged, fear of impacting your children and financial concerns. Managing the divorce and all its consequences becomes yet another thing on your mind, above and beyond your professional and family responsibilities.

It is easy for someone going through a divorce to get so wrapped up in the logistics and turmoil of the changes they are experiencing that they forget to take care of themselves. Rightly so, many people prioritise their children's wellbeing during divorce. But one must ask: can you be the best parent for your children if you are not standing strong? In this context, prioritising your own self-care is not an act of selfishness, it is essential to giving you the strength and resilience required to get you and your family through divorce.

"Holding on to anger is like drinking poison and expecting the other person to die."

Buddha

---

[28] In 1967, psychiatrists Thomas Holmes and Richard Rahe examined the medical records of over 5,000 medical patients as a way to determine whether stressful events might cause illnesses. Patients were asked to tally a list of 43 life events based on a relative score. Their results were published as the Social Readjustment Rating Scale (SRRS), known more commonly as the Holmes and Rahe Stress Scale.

1 RECONNECT WITH WHAT MAKES YOU HAPPY

While divorce is often a sad time for everyone involved, it can also be an opportunity. Anyone who has been married will know that it is not uncommon for individuals to give up certain interests or hobbies during marriage, be it because family life took over or because their spouse didn't share the same passion. Divorce is a unique opportunity to reengage in the activities that bring you joy. With most divorces ending up with some division of time spent with the children, you now have an ideal setup to use that space for activities that are important solely to you. Now is the time to bring out that dusty yoga mat, the old canvases and paint brushes, or that overpriced bread machine you never used and dive back in! You're likely to find great relief in a few hours spent not thinking about your divorce, your kids or work. But especially, you will regain a sense of who you are and give yourself the greatest gift of all: doing things you truly enjoy.

> "I was trying so hard not to disappoint anyone, I forgot about what made me happy."
>
> *Julia Roberts in Eat Pray Love*

EXPERT TIP

It isn't uncommon for my clients to struggle with their newfound independence and to find it challenging to figure out what they truly stand for. As one client recently put it "I haven't made a decision by myself in 18 years, I don't know what I want anymore". One small initial exercise you can do to help you reconnect with yourself is to draw a list of 20 things that you have been wanting to do but that you didn't pursue because your spouse didn't agree. It can be watching a movie that had caught your eye, tasting a new sort of cuisine, having breakfast in bed on Sundays or even going on a trip somewhere you've always wanted to visit. Draw up a list of these 20 items and make it a goal to complete all 20 items within a year. This is a great bite-size first step towards redefining your tastes and embracing your own way of experiencing life, outside of your spouse's influence.

② STOP THINKING OF DIVORCE AS A FAILURE

While it is common for people to refer to divorce as a failed marriage, it is important to shift the narrative to describing it as a successful new start. You will often notice that those who are most critical of your personal decisions are those who have not had the courage to fix their own broken lives. By judging you, they are justifying their own choices. Staying in a bad relationship is not what takes courage and strength, it is recognising its end that should be valued and acknowledged. The guilt that might come from the hurt inflicted on your children can seem unavoidable, but what about the damage caused by being raised in a conflictual household? What example do you want to set for them? Would you want your children to live their own lives in that way or would you rather they have the courage to accept that their marriage isn't working and move on?

People often underestimate the strength of character it takes to choose happiness over an unfulfilling relationship. Even if you were not the one who decided to divorce, it is worth wondering whether you really would have wanted to remain in a marriage where the other person wasn't happy. So, shift your narrative. Change the words you use. Divorce is a second chance at love, and often at life, which you have had the courage to embrace!

3 PRACTISE SELF-CARE AND SELF-LOVE DURING AND AFTER YOUR DIVORCE

Whether you are getting divorced or not, you should always be your own best friend. Your value and sense of self is not defined by another person or by your marital status, it is defined by you. If you are struggling to feel good about yourself, you can try practising daily affirmations that will remind you of your value and qualities.

Be aware of the situations in which you feel the most vulnerable and schedule your self-care activities at those times, when you need an extra boost. Do you feel blue right after dropping off the children at your ex-spouse's house for the weekend? On Sunday evenings? On Friday nights when you used to all sit together and watch a movie and have pizza? Whatever the trigger, these times are opportunities to turn a negative experience into a morale-boosting one.

As time passes and you come out of your divorce feeling confident and supported, you will suddenly realise that you have created new traditions for yourself that will continue to help you stand strong for years to come.

Conclusion

Having reached the end of this book, you've likely come to realise the immense value of preparation when facing divorce. The journey is complex and challenging, but you are now better equipped to handle it with more confidence. As Benjamin Franklin wisely said, "By failing to prepare, you are preparing to fail." This sentiment rings especially true in divorce, where the emotional and financial stakes are high.

This book has aimed to do more than just offer facts and guidance. It has sought to reshape how you approach divorce, empowering you to take control of your circumstances and avoid many of the pitfalls that could otherwise cause harm.

Reflecting on the journey so far

Throughout this book, I have shared lessons learned from both personal experience and professional insight. My story began with a divorce that left me feeling overwhelmed, unprepared, and uncertain of my next steps. Since then, I have learned that preparation can drastically alter the experience. One of the hardest lessons for anyone going through divorce is recognising that while you cannot control everything, you can control how well-prepared you are to face the challenges ahead.

I hope that by reading this book, you now have the tools to avoid some of the same mistakes I made and can move forward with a clearer sense of direction and self-leadership.

The value of preparation

As you will have clearly heard me say throughout this book, preparation is an essential requirement to ensure you maintain control of your divorce rather than let it get out of hand and "happen to you". Thinking long term will allow you to get past the immediate emotional reactions you might be experiencing and to focus on a thought-through and fully considered plan. Let's reflect on some key areas where preparation has the most profound impact:

DEBUNKING MYTHS AND MISCONCEPTIONS

Many people enter divorce proceedings with misconceptions that can shape their actions and decisions. In the first chapter, we explored some of the most common divorce myths, such as assumptions about child arrangements, financial settlements, or the idea that you cannot back out of divorce once it's started. Understanding these truths early on will enable you to make informed decisions based on facts rather than assumptions.

EMOTIONAL READINESS

Divorce is more than a legal process; it's an emotional journey. Preparing yourself emotionally by setting realistic expectations, understanding your spouse's conflict style, and seeking the right support networks are crucial to maintaining resilience throughout the divorce. By taking time to reflect on your emotional needs, you'll be better able to manage the inevitable challenges ahead.

CHOOSING THE RIGHT DIVORCE PATH

There are multiple ways to approach divorce, and not all are right for every couple. We explored the benefits of mediation, collaborative law, and arbitration. The option you choose can have a significant impact on the outcome of your divorce. Careful consideration of these options can lead to a more amicable separation, which in turn can reduce both the emotional and financial toll.

GATHERING THE RIGHT INFORMATION AND TEAM

Before initiating the legal proceedings, it is essential to be organised. This means gathering financial documents and assembling a team of professionals: a lawyer, a Certified Divorce Coach®, a financial adviser, and perhaps a therapist. By taking these steps from the outset, you are well-positioned to make sound decisions. This also helps avoid delays or last-minute scrambles for critical information that could derail your plans.

FINANCIAL PLANNING

One of the most significant sources of stress during and after divorce is its financial impact. We've discussed the importance of budgeting for both the immediate costs of divorce and the long-term financial implications, such as whether you can afford to keep the family home or how to manage ongoing expenses such as school fees. Financial planning helps you avoid being caught off guard by unexpected expenses and allows you to create a more secure future for yourself and your family.

PREPARING FOR DIFFICULT CONVERSATIONS

How you communicate your divorce to family and friends can shape the support you receive. Whether it's telling your spouse, your children, or your extended family, approaching these conversations with care and preparation is vital. We explored how to prepare for these emotionally charged discussions and the importance of safety and wellbeing, especially if you are an expatriate or facing difficult circumstances. Preparing for these conversations helps you manage their emotional weight and maintain important relationships.

"Peace is not the absence of conflict, but the ability to cope with it."

Mahatma Gandhi

Moving forward with confidence

As underlined in this book, thorough preparation not only helps you avoid mistakes but also establishes a sense of control throughout the divorce. When you are clear about your priorities, realistic about your finances, and deliberate in your emotional and legal strategies, the path through divorce becomes more manageable.

Nonetheless, keep in mind the saying: "You plan, God laughs". The nature of plans is that they don't always go according to plan. So keep an open mind and be flexible. Things might not unfold exactly as you anticipated – there are two of you in this dance after all – but if you remain steady and consistent, you will manage to pivot without losing sight of your long-term objectives. In other words, the road might be windier than expected, but it will still lead to the same destination.

I encourage you to revisit the boxes with the most common mistakes and exercises included in this book. These tools will continue to serve you as you navigate divorce and begin the next chapter of your life.

A final thought: preparation is empowerment

By planning your divorce, you are not just surviving the process, you are laying the groundwork for a future that aligns with your values, aspirations, and long-term goals. In short, you are offering yourself the essential ingredients of empowerment.

As you close this book, let me take a moment to wish you strength, resilience, and peace of mind as you move forward into the next phase of your life, ready to embrace new beginnings.

Can I ask you a small favour?

Please leave me a helpful review on Amazon to help me make the next version of this book even better.

Your input will be invaluable to other people as they start their own divorce journey.

Acknowledgements

This book began its journey during a conversation with my mother. It was her idea that I bring together the diverse topics I regularly address in my articles into a single, cohesive volume. As I mulled over her suggestion, the concept gradually took shape. We spent hours brainstorming the right structure for the book. I eventually landed on the idea of building it around the most common questions people ask at the outset of their divorce journey, addressing their fears, misconceptions, and uncertainties.

I owe an enormous debt of gratitude to my mother, who was the driving force behind this book and gave me the courage to take the leap into writing it. Her unwavering encouragement, coupled with her sharp insights and thoughtful feedback, proved invaluable throughout the process. She not only inspired me to begin but also supported me every step of the way, reviewing countless drafts and offering constructive input.

I also want to extend my heartfelt thanks to my friends and collaborators who generously gave their time to review the manuscript and share their perspectives. Their comments, suggestions, and keen observations helped refine and improve the book, ensuring that it would be as clear, practical, and helpful as possible. This collective effort has been instrumental in shaping a resource I hope will resonate with readers and provide real value during what is often a challenging period in their lives.

THANK YOU

Ambar Bharwani, Anna Sharp, Anne Hearon-Armstrong, Annie Rodgers, Astrid Le Vern, Ayse Valentin, Caroline Gaudron, Cecile Pons, Dorothee Cointreau Slovic, Helen Biscoe-Taylor, Ian Lovatt, Isabelle Veyrat-Masson, Karen Omand, Katy Harris, Lucy Greenwood, Marie-Laure Vercambre, Melissa Lesson, Paula Crowhurst, Peter Burgess, Sandrine Mercy, Stephanie Kulas, Sofia Neves, Rebecca Hawkins and Victoria Mendrzyk.

To my readers, this book is for you. It is written with the hope that it will equip you with the tools and understanding to navigate the complexities of divorce thoughtfully and purposefully. My wish is that it enables you to transform this life-changing moment into an opportunity for a fresh start rather than a destructive experience for you, your children, and your wider family.

Finally, I am reminded that a book is rarely a solitary endeavour. While the words on these pages bear my name, they reflect the shared wisdom, encouragement, and kindness of those around me. To all who contributed, knowingly or unknowingly, thank you.

Printed in Great Britain
by Amazon

59488702R00138